ROUTLEDGE LIBRARY EDITIONS: SPECIAL EDUCATIONAL NEEDS

Volume 27

PROBLEM BEHAVIOUR IN THE SECONDARY SCHOOL

PROBLEM BEHAVIOUR IN THE SECONDARY SCHOOL

A Systems Approach

Edited by
BILL GILLHAM

Routledge
Taylor & Francis Group

LONDON AND NEW YORK

First published in 1981 by Croom Helm Ltd

This edition first published in 2019
by Routledge
2 Park Square, Milton Park, Abingdon, Oxon OX14 4RN

and by Routledge
711 Third Avenue, New York, NY 10017

Routledge is an imprint of the Taylor & Francis Group, an informa business

British Library Cataloguing in Publication Data
A catalogue record for this book is available from the British Library

ISBN: 978-1-138-58532-4 (Set)
ISBN: 978-0-429-46809-4 (Set) (ebk)
ISBN: 978-1-138-58772-4 (Volume 27) (hbk)
ISBN: 978-0-429-50379-5 (Volume 27) (ebk)

Publisher's Note
The publisher has gone to great lengths to ensure the quality of this
reprint but points out that some imperfections in the original copies
may be apparent.

Disclaimer
The publisher has made every effort to trace copyright holders and
would welcome correspondence from those they have been unable to
trace.

Problem Behaviour in the Secondary School

A SYSTEMS APPROACH

EDITED BY BILL GILLHAM

CROOM HELM LONDON

Croom Helm Ltd, 2-10 St John's Road, London SW11

British Library Cataloguing in Publication Data

Problem behaviour in the secondary school.
    1. Classroom management
    2. Education, Secondary
    I. Gillham, Bill
    373.1'1'02   LB3013

    ISBN 0-7099-0129-1
    ISBN 0-7099-1102-5 Pbk

Printed and bound in Great Britain by
Biddles Ltd, Guildford and King's Lynn

CONTENTS

PREFATORY NOTE

This book attempts to draw together a theoretical and empirical basis
for a systems approach to reducing behaviour problems in school, as an
alternative to the traditional solutions of 'treatment' and 'placement'
which have been rejected by many psychologists and teachers in recent
years. It aims to show that not only are many problems of 'maladjustment' really problems of low achievement and difficult social relationships
within the large institution, but that schools themselves are probably
the best therapists we have.

The contributors come from varied professional backgrounds, but all
with a direct interest in education, and all actively concerned with the
reformulation of practice.

I am grateful to Judith Gillham and Margaret Grainger for editorial and
clerical help in the preparation of the manuscript; and to the Controller
of Her Majesty's Stationery Office for permission to reproduce or
derive from Crown copyright tables appearing in Chapter 6.

B.G.

1 RETHINKING THE PROBLEM*

Bill Gillham

There was a point in the early seventies when it seemed as if many secondary schools in the major urban areas were heading for breakdown, and it is likely that some schools came dangerously near it. A special news report in the *Times Educational Supplement* for 8 October 1971 was headed 'Secondary School Crisis' and presented a disturbing picture of increasing absenteeism, educational failure and anti-social behaviour. 'For those teaching in our inner city schools,' ran the first paragraph of a report on classroom violence, 'it is an everyday reality, a subject of regular, bewildered staffroom discussion.' Even allowing for a journalist's sense of the dramatic there can be little doubt that it reflected the atmosphere of confusion that many teachers found themselves in at that time.

It would strike a note of false optimism to suggest that the picture at the beginning of the eighties is radically improved. Secondary schools can still be stressful and unsatisfactory places to work in, but the general situation is better than might have been predicted. There are some encouraging trends in practice, and new evidence about the positive effects of schooling in the face of social difficulties which has forced a reconsideration of accepted evidence to the contrary. Perhaps most important of all, there has been a shift in our perceptions of problems of behaviour and social relationships in secondary schools. This last development – rethinking the problem – makes it possible to consider solutions in different terms from the traditional 'cures' which have been found to be inadequate. The problem of anti-social behaviour is still with us but the broad characteristics of constructive action, and some of the details, are becoming apparent; there is no longer a general impression that schools are unable to cope. At the same time the situation is far from secure and there is some ground to be regained.

In particular, the suspicion that schools might be impotent in the face of social problems has been a damaging influence on public and professional confidence in education. It was ironic that comprehensive

*This chapter is based on a paper given at the Annual Conference of the Scottish Association of Local Government and Educational Psychologists held at the University of Glasgow in April 1980.

schools, established on the basis of social idealism, at one time looked like failing in social terms because of poor relationships between children and their teachers as well as between children themselves. Reactions to this process were various, including the liberal notion of 'deschooling' which further undermined faith in the effectiveness of schools. But the more general response was a hardening of teachers' attitudes, involving a loss of goodwill that has not yet been recovered. The rather strident reaction from teacher unions in the early seventies was an understandable defence of teachers under great pressure. Cox (1977) in an investigation of stress in teachers in Clwyd Education Authority found that absence was often related to anxiety about discipline and classroom confrontation situations. Although focused on these problems, the malaise of teachers can be related to the insecurity of their circumstances and the discouragement of prevailing attitudes.

And the prevailing attitude at the beginning of the last decade was that schools could not hope to do much in the face of adverse home circumstances and social environments. As is often the case with long-term, large-scale plans, by the time comprehensive reorganisation was becoming generally established the atmosphere of social optimism in which it was conceived had been replaced by doubts about schools as agents of social change. Thus many teachers and pupils were having to cope with radical changes in school organisation, sometimes hastily arranged and without adequate consultation, in a climate of opinion that expected little to come out of the process.

The 'doomwatch' educational sociology of the sixties, although by no means universally accepted, had had considerable popular impact on the profession. An article by Basil Bernstein (1970) in *New Society* entitled 'Education Cannot Compensate for Society' (which is surely correct) none the less represented a view that was widely over-interpreted. The much-quoted Jencks Report (1972) which analysed a vast amount of data relating to home and school influences on attainment (including the earlier (1966) Coleman report) concluded that 'equalising the quality of high schools would reduce cognitive inequalities by one per cent or less' – and much more on the same theme. The Coleman Report had concluded that educational attainment was largely independent of schooling received. The fact that these conclusions have not stood up to more recent careful scrutiny (see Chapter 3) did not lessen their impact at the time. It is some kind of tribute to the idealism of those working in our secondary schools that they kept faith with themselves to the extent they did: it is very difficult to remain motivated when the accepted wisdom is that your

efforts are of no avail. Abstract moralising about the negative or punitive
attitudes teachers have sometimes displayed towards their charges fails to
recognise the extent to which they have had to cope, unsupported, with the
anti-social or unco-operative behaviour of children who were themselves
often reacting to the unsatisfactory nature of the school system.

Nor was there much help for schools from outside agencies. If we exclude
legally defined delinquency and the formal processes that are erected to manage it, the main provision for helping troubled and troublesome children in
school has been the Child Guidance Service and a restricted number of
schools for the 'maladjusted'. At that time, however, Child Guidance was
having its own crisis of effectiveness, a crisis apparently justified by the
evidence. An epidemiological study of schoolchildren in Buckinghamshire
by Shepherd *et al.* (1971) comparing children rated as 'deviant' on a range of
behaviours revealed that, over a three-year period, those who received
Child Guidance treatment showed identical rates of improvement to those
who did not. It must be noted that this study has not gone unchallenged
(Rutter 1972), although very similar data on improvement and 'recovery'
rates were presented in a survey of American studies (Levitt 1957, 1971) as
well as in reviews of treatment with adults (Eysenck 1952; Fix and Haffke
1976). But, effective or not, Child Guidance was in any case irrelevant to
the problem of difficult behaviour in school in another way. Its generally expressed purpose was the treatment of 'neurotic' disorders in
children, i.e. anxiety, withdrawal and so on; it being presumed that
behaviour difficulties were usually considered to be 'social problems'
or to be 'acting out' their conflicts and so unsuitable for therapy aimed
at achieving 'insight'. The following quotation from the 1975 Annual
Report of a Child Guidance Clinic in a London Borough spells this out
quite clearly:

> Behaviour Disorder/Anti-social Disorder now makes up 70% of
> referrals for 1974-75 but in previous years was 60%. These are the
> children who make life difficult for their teachers, their parents and
> society generally. Many warrant referral to the Child Guidance
> Service, but many contravene the law and require those sanctions
> that society has deemed appropriate for their misdemeanours. It is
> unrealistic to refer large, acting-out delinquents who lack insight and
> do not wish for insight into their behaviour. *The Child Guidance
> Service has little to offer in such cases.* (my italics)

Child Guidance, with its long waiting lists, its slow and cumbersome
mode of action, its physically remote context, and its preoccupation

with psychoanalytic explanation and protracted therapy, became a byword for ineffectuality. It is not surprising that educational psychologists, the only members of the Child Guidance 'team' to go regularly into schools, and therefore most conscious of the inadequacy of the service, have progressively disentangled themselves from it. During the past decade independent school psychological services have become the norm: but this trend has not always been accompanied by the development of more adequate ways of working. We return to this theme later.

If the conventional helping services were of no substantial help, LEAs still had to take some positive action in the face of rising suspension-rates and the militancy of teacher unions. What happened was the unplanned and unco-ordinated, but fairly general development of 'withdrawal' units for children presenting behaviour problems. The characteristics of these units and the implications of their development are considered at length in Chapters 5 and 7 but it is no over-simplification to see their purpose as a kind of disposal mechanism. This is a criticism at one level only: if there do not seem to be any good solutions it is hardly surprising when bad solutions take their place. The units that were first established soon filled up and there was a demand for more. We can see now that this was a policy of infinite regress; as Arno Rabinowitz comments in Chapter 5, 'in this way many problems of behaviour are apparently coped with, more are created, fewer are solved'.

If the situation has changed it must be emphasised that the change is 'in process' and complex, with many strands to it. The critical scrutiny of schools by 'external' elements in our society – from central government to individual parents – has engendered a degree of self-criticism in schools that is leading to internal developments of some significance. At a time when the mood of society is critical of the achievements of education and demands accountability in this respect, there is little sympathy for schools that try to displace their problems outwards. But the profession is better equipped to deal with the tough-mindedness of accountability than it was a decade ago. A major element is that of experience: large comprehensive secondary schools have now been running for a long time and there are more teachers with the relevant experience in running them. Formal management training has been only a minor element in this because managing a school is some-thing of a unique enterprise and can only really be learnt by doing it. Organising a school to meet the needs of a much wider range of children makes different demands at all levels on the staff involved and requires a period of adjustment. For example, Galloway (1976) investigating truancy and suspensions in Sheffield secondary schools, found that comprehensive schools based on old grammar schools suspended the most pupils, indicating that attitudes to, and handling of children were factors in the problems that were encountered. More than that, one could say that the perceptions and behaviour of staff in part created the problem. This may seem like 'blaming' the teachers (and note how unacceptable that is), but that would be a misconstruction; problems of social behaviour are problems of relationships, they occur between people rather than within them. The expectations of traditional grammar school teachers are not easily accommodated to the behaviour of non-academic, working-class children. That conflicts occur is the fault of neither group; but the initiative for dealing with the situation does lie mainly with the teacher.

The behavioural effects of changes in teacher behaviour/attitude and is what goes on inside a school – the situation where pupil and teacher have to get on with each other – is as demonstrably true as it is intuitively doubtful. The reality is the difficult child: it requires a great feat of imagination to conceive that things could have been different especially when, as is frequently the case, he continues his anti-social career. Certainly some forms of problem behaviour – especially delinquency – *once established* seem to develop a maintaining power of their own which runs down only gradually, the best form of help being to minimise the damage the adolescent is doing to himself and others during this phase. In the case of problem behaviour within school, however, it may be more pertinent to ask: what in the school situation is helping to maintain the behaviour? In a well-defined institution like a school the (good or bad) behaviour of individuals is, to some extent, kept going by the task and role demands on them, so that anti-social behaviour can be supported by the institution itself. This 'maintenance' factor is demonstrated most simply by moving a child to another school (not necessarily a special school). Thus, in one situation you can find a child who is said to be very 'maladjusted', who becomes quite different (and much less 'maladjusted') after a straight-forward transfer – provided that the new teachers have a positive, or at least a neutral attitude to the transferring pupil. Having prepared many detailed and careful reports on a child's maladjustment, a common experience for the writer has been to find that the receiving school did not recognise the child in my report: they were quite right not to do so. The positive lesson from this is that modifications within the original school *might* have achieved what was brought about only by a change of school, although it is important not to underestimate the inertia of established attitudes towards a child who is perceived as a 'problem'.

Prospective pessimism has some justification – especially if we cannot change circumstances. Less justifiable is the intuitive conviction that the child was bound to end up being difficult or delinquent because of his home environment and his early experiences. There is good evidence that this process of determination is not a necessary one; and that the school he attends is an important factor in whether or not a child becomes 'maladjusted' or 'delinquent', its influence extending out beyond the boundaries of the school. This may sound like an exaggerated claim and it is, indeed, important not to overstate it. Education is particularly prone to tiresome swings in fashion and emphasis. But in the area of school influence on behaviour there is a need for a reassertion of the significance of that role.

The importance of the school as an agent of behaviour change, as a means of preventing problem behaviour, is something that has been actively rediscovered only recently. It is, of course, in marked contrast to the prevailing view of only a few years ago. Referring to the standpoint of contemporary sociological investigations, Phillipson (1971) comments:

> The implicit suggestion is that all schools are sufficiently alike to produce a standardised response from their pupils. The idea that there may be considerable differences between overtly similar schools . . . does not seem to have occurred to writers on delinquency.
> (p. 239)

School, in this view was a neutral backcloth against which pupil behaviour was acted out in terms of home background and individual psychological history. Certainly school was not seen as a *major* influence on behaviour: the sociological trend was against it. These fashions in attitude and interpretation mean that evidence is neglected even when it is there.

Two studies in the late sixties pointed to the influence of school on anti-social behaviour, irrespective of intake and catchment area – those of Power *et al.* (1967) and Clegg and Megson (1968).

Power and his colleagues looked at indices of problem behaviour amongst secondary modern schoolchildren in the then London Borough of Tower Hamlets. They found wide differences including, for example, delinquency rates varying from 7 to 77 per 1000 children in schools taking a very similar population. The importance of this was that, quite apart from differences within schools themselves, they seemed to exert an influence on pupil behaviour *outside* of school. Unfortunately Power published his findings in such a way (and under the heading *Delinquent Schools?*) that it appeared to be a blame-shifting exercise. Understandably the response from the local authority and the teacher unions was defensive. This was a pity because although it could be argued that the schools with the high rates were failing, a more constructive, and probably fairer view would be that some schools were remarkably successful at *preventing* delinquency in vulnerable children – succeeding where other agencies were failing. Of course, one could take the view that delinquency is not the concern of schools since it principally occurs off school premises. But improved behaviour in school and out probably reflects a common set of attitudes and practices on the part of the headteacher and his staff.

This is apparent in the study by Clegg and Megson, incorporated in a book entitled *Children in Distress*, published in 1968, and remarkable for its idealism and commitment to the effectiveness of schools, a commitment based on a life-time's practical experience since the senior author was for many years the Chief Education Officer for what was then the West Riding of Yorkshire. He argues that school must be the major influence on children outside the home:

> Every child spends about one-quarter of his waking hours in school . . . For something like 1400 hours each year he is in the company of teachers and groups of his peers who are likely to know him better than anyone outside his circle of close relations and intimate friends . . . Moreover, the school stands in a different relationship from any other public service to the generality of children. The medical officer or the children's officer or the NSPCC or other welfare agencies may on occasion have to say 'The law does not permit me to help this child.' The school, on the other hand, is breaking the law if it does not endeavour to help the child on five days each week for some forty weeks in the year. For the mass of distressed youngsters, that is those whose distress stops short of the law or of official protection, the only source of help may be the school. (p. 40)

Clegg quite clearly sees the *prevention* of future difficulties as a major influence emanating from the school.

'How can a school make a bad child good?' [he asks.] 'Why do some

schools which draw on bad social areas manage to steer clear of
juvenile crime? Is there any truth in the assertion that a good school
can raise the social standard of the whole area in which it is situated,
and, if so, how does this happen?'

Clegg presents his own answer by describing a process of comprehensive
change in one West Riding school. He gives an account of how a wide
range of behaviour problems in school were progressively brought
under control with parallel improvements in behaviour outside of
school. He concludes:

> the significant thing is that during the few years in which these
> activities were being introduced into a new school the delinquency
> rate was reduced markedly and a school which was certainly the most
> notorious in the county became one of the most respected; and the
> change was certainly significant enough to be noticed with consider-
> able satisfaction by the police. (p. 131)

The only dissatisfaction one feels in reading this account is that the
process of change comes across as somewhat mysterious and dependent
upon the charisma of a new headmaster (evidently well supported by
his CEO!). But this does not alter the scale of the achievement. Properly
organised and properly supported, a school can be a real agent of social
change. At the level of the individual child it means that the school can
be a particularly effective therapist.

   This implication also emerged from a study carried out, from a
different viewpoint, by the psychiatrist Dennis Gath and his colleagues
(Gath *et al.* 1977). They were concerned to investigate the take-up of
child guidance services in the London Borough of Croydon and concluded that 'changes in the educational system afford the best hope for
coping with maladjustment among schoolchildren'. Noting that causal
research in child psychiatry has tended to concentrate on intra-psychic
and intra-familial factors they comment that 'future research in child
psychiatry might profitably pay more regard to the wider social
environment of the child . . .'

   The findings of their investigation parallel those of Power and Clegg.

> Establishments of low status within the educational system were
> found to have high child-guidance and delinquency rates: whether
> this finding reflected a selective process or a greater exposure to risk
> for some children could not be decided on the evidence, though the

inter-school variation was independent of neighbourhood effects. As in the Tower Hamlets study (Power *et al.* 1967), disparities between neighbouring schools were so large as to suggest that major factors must operate within the individual school.

The elucidation of this problem is too urgent for it to be neglected or set aside, either by the educational authorities or by the teaching profession. If it be established that the school exercises an independent influence on the risks of maladjustment and of delinquency, the nature of this influence must be explored by further research. (p. 114)

Gath cites an unpublished study by Reade (1971) comparing high and low delinquency-rate schools in Manchester which revealed marked differences in policy and attitude between the two groups:

Those working in the low-rate schools, who typically believed that much could be done to counteract any unfavourable home environ- ment, had established contact with many of the parents and were aware both of the children's home backgrounds and of the parents' attitudes; they also appreciated the need for social support of problem families. In all these respects they differed from their colleagues in the high-rate schools. (p. 115)

This study bears comparison with Clegg's and Megsons's account where the community involvement of the head was a major factor in the achievement of change. The external influence of a school is evidently not some spiritual transfer effect but the outcome of active involvement.

The identification of those processes and characteristics of schools which predispose 'good' outcomes in terms of behaviour and attainments have been explored and identified more fully by Reynolds (1976) and, in particular, by Rutter *et al.* (1979). These investigations are given full consideration in Chapters 3 and 4 of the present book but it is important to note that both studies found that successful schools were not necessarily those with 'external' advantages like better buildings and other resources. It was 'internal' characteristics that determined standards of behaviour and attainments. In other words, the school is very much part of the psychology of the child – at least while he's there.

One of the peculiarities of the traditional approach to difficult children in schools is that the problem has almost always been defined as the child and, more or less prominently, his home background. When referring to the Child Guidance or School Psychological Service, schools have typically been expected to provide comprehensive details of the child, his family, his attainments, his offences, and so on. This is then followed up by a detailed examination of the child and his parents; by such means reasons can always be found for difficult behaviour. But this sort of examination rarely contributes to effective change and it cannot, of course, be preventive. By definition a preventive service must operate before problems occur. However, even if one could identify potentially delinquent or anti-social children – and this is possible to some extent, although not as often as hindsight would lead us to believe – such individual identification still leaves us with the question of what effective preventive action we can take (see Chapter 6).

The implication of the studies briefly reviewed so far is that preventive action, especially for problems in school, is best taken at the level of the school as institution and the management skills of individual teachers. Such a perspective is still somewhat alien to our thinking about troublesome children in school. If we could get rid of the trouble-makers (which we can't) then everything would be all right. There can be few teachers (including the writer) who have not felt like that about unco-operative children in a class. But practicality apart, most recognise that such a viewpoint is neither fair nor humane. It is not fair because the evidence is that schools are themselves a factor in the difficult behaviour of their pupils; and it is not humane because any disposal is likely to have adverse effects on the child. The persistent definition of the child as the problem can be seen as one aspect of the limited rights of children. With other, more powerful, groups such explanations and actions are not acceptable. As I have recently written elsewhere (Gillham 1980), the operation of another explanatory model can be seen by direct analogy:

> This model is already in operation in another sector of our society which is also made up of hierarchically organised institutions of people, namely, the factories and offices of commerce. The people who run these institutions commonly have problems with their work force and can call on occupational psychologists to help them. Neither the managers nor the psychologists think in terms of 'mal-adjusted' workers nor do they seek to explain their difficult behaviour in terms of their home backgrounds; and the personnel manager who suggested that a worker should see a psychologist for treatment would probably find himself in a very difficult situation. Depending on the

problem, the occupational psychologist will look at such things as:

(a) communications within the factory;
(b) whether workers are getting fair recognition of their needs and achievements;
(c) whether there are difficulties for the foremen in carrying out some of their supervisory functions;
(d) whether the tasks are well-suited to individual workers; and so on.

It is an axiom of management practice that trouble with employees is always the fault of the management. This is no more fair to managers than saying that anti-social behaviour by children in school (or outside it) is the fault of the teachers. *But it leads to more constructive action than the vilification of workers or schoolchildren.*

The argument is not that unco-operative adult workers or school-age children are simply created by their work or school environment: home backgrounds and individual predispositions will make them individually more or less vulnerable. There is no question but that these background factors are of great importance: it would be so much easier if we had to teach only children who came to school literate, motivated to learn, considerate in their social behaviour. But at present there is little that we can do directly to affect adverse social environments and their psychological consequences at the neighbourhood level. Gath (1977) comments 'in the present state of our society, the prospects for improving bad schools are better than those for improving bad neighbourhoods'. However, even the influence of bad neighbourhoods can be mitigated by altering the *balance of intake* for particular schools. Rutter *et al.* (1979) found that the social class and attainment balance was an important factor in enabling school influence to operate, especially in relation to delinquency (see also Eggleston 1977). But, in any case, for those children predisposed by social or psychological factors to be 'difficult' what happens in school is crucial. To a considerable extent, whether they actually *manifest* difficulties depends on the situations they encounter there. And in reactive effect, the pattern of social behaviour maintained by the institution may then influence the predispositions of the individual. If it is a truism that we are all formed and maintained by our social experiences, the implications are not always perceived in practice. Changes in our circumstances change us superficially or profoundly, and the effects can be harmful or beneficial.

An example from the research literature illustrates this point in

relation to children. During the 1960s Rutter *et al.* (1970) carried out
an epidemiological study of a wide range of health and behaviour
problems in the Isle of Wight. Amongst other things, they asked the
parents and teachers of over 2,000 children in the age-range 10-11 years
to complete a check-list indicative of behavioural and emotional
problems. Those children who had more than a certain number of items
checked (about 13 per cent of the total) were then interviewed by
psychiatrists and further information was obtained about them. It was
finally decided that 118 (5.4 per cent) of the children could be
considered as having a behavioural or neurotic disorder (or both). Of
these, teachers and parents had identified about the same number of
children *but by and large they had selected different children.* The
actual correlation between the groups was +0.18. In part this difference
was due to the fact that teachers reported more behavioural problems
whilst parents reported more emotional problems. This is unlikely to be
just a matter of differing criteria; it is more probable that, as Rutter
concludes, the situation (which includes the people involved and the
nature of the relationship) was a major factor in the 'disorder'. For a
child to manifest difficult behaviour or emotional upset a number of
things have to come together: the child's attitudes and vulnerabilities
on the one hand; on the other how he is handled and the demands that
are made on him.

Regarded as a function of differences in role and setting, such a
finding seems unexceptional enough; but the implications are not usually
applied to our own commonsense experience at the *interpersonal* level.
One of the things that commonsense tells us is that the person we know,
in the relationship that we have with them, is the 'real' person and that
the characteristics they display with us are what they are 'really' like.
But, of course, we only know them in the restriction of our relationship and usually in a restricted context – be it as spouse, employer,
golfer, pupil or offspring. It is almost always surprising – and curiously
unacceptable – to find that their behaviour with others is quite different
and that other people have a quite different view of them. Indeed, when
we encounter this we often try to persuade the others to share our
view (observe the process, anytime, in the staffroom discussion of a
child someone finds 'difficult'). The disinclination to recognise our
own role in how others behave means that our tendency in interpersonal relations is to make it difficult for them to change. So that
although we may 'want' people to be different we may, at the same
time, not enable them to be so. For example, cynicism about a
'problem' child's ability to behave differently is part of the social

process that keeps him in a deviant role. We tend to stereotype people and then, unconsciously, attempt to keep them in that stereotype. What all this means is that individuals, *if they are allowed*, have some potential for change – and this extends even to middle-aged schoolteachers and psychologists. But we have first to admit the possibility that, for example, a child handled differently might be, not just a more manageable child, but perhaps sufficiently different as to be no longer a problem. It requires a shift in our thinking and the development of a range of skills to bring it about, whether as a teacher or as someone who helps teachers.

The implication for the educational psychologist is that his focus of attention has got to shift from the child to the teacher and the school. His traditional style of working does not enable him to do this. When a problem has reached the stage where the school feel they can no longer cope – at which point the child is usually referred – the psychologist can do nothing except tidy up the mess; and he cannot always do that. Since he normally only visits the school in response to a referral, and then only briefly, the situation perpetuates itself. It is comparatively easy and relatively quick to investigate the child, more difficult and more time-consuming (in the short run) to investigate the school. It can also be more threatening both to the school and the psychologist. Consider the following quotation from a summary of a discussion amongst educational psychologists of the Northern Branch of the BPS Division of Educational and Child Psychology. They were discussing a paper by the sociologist David Hargreaves on the interactionist view of children's problems in school:

> Some people felt that moves towards a less child-centred approach to work in schools would be fraught with difficulty. Psychologists worked with their employing authority and with other education department staff, and there was a great danger of conflict in these relationships if their role was to change. The relationships with schools and school staffs depended on credibility, and this credibility was best achieved by giving the school answers in terms of the child's deviance. (*Occasional Papers of the DECP*, Summer 1977, p. 556)

Whilst it would be naïve in the extreme to suggest that there would not be some conflict and resistance to the development of school-centred rather than child-centred activities, all that can be said is that those psychologists who have tried it, have not found it such a fearsome experience (see Chapter 10, and Miller (1980)). In any case, schools themselves have for some time been taking a look at their structure, policy and teacher support systems without much external help.

The above quotation is about the professional anxiety of some educational psychologists; their training and their conventional experience have not equipped them for a role that is becoming necessary. Fortunately not all psychologists are as negative. Topping (1979) comments: 'If we have no skills in changing organisations, then we will have to learn them' and he points to the extensive literature on organisational psychology, as yet mainly related to the institutions of government and industry. In two separate papers in the same journal, Taylor (1979) and Fawcett (1979) both refer to the need for psychologists to study schools as social institutions. Fawcett emphasises the special validity of this in relation to the individual case: in simple form this may well express the style of working which the educational psychologist needs to evolve. In particular, it avoids the danger of thinking about children in notional terms – and thereby neglecting individual perceptions, meanings and attitudes (see Chapter 11).

Most educational psychologists, like the writer, took up their profession because of their concern about the difficulties of individual children: few of them want to change that sense of priorities. Where we have failed has not been at the level of concern but at the level of *action.* In particular, we have failed to follow through the problems of the individual child as an indication of a more general need for change – so that we don't find other children in the same situation in the future. The actions we have usually initiated have typically been too short term, too restricted, too remote from the context of the problem – clinic-based treatment, withdrawal remedial teaching, narrowly focused behaviour modification – without affecting the everyday character of what the child experiences in school which must be a major determinant of his behaviour and emotions whilst he is there (Tizard 1976).

But where does the psychologist begin? A beginning is to visit schools on a regular time-contracted basis rather than in response to open-ended referrals. As a way of working this is now fairly common and sufficiently long established for it to be evaluated. It can be no more than a method for controlling referrals from schools and it is possible for the psychologist to do a traditional job, carrying his clinic round on his back and setting it up in the Medical Inspection room in each school he visits. But it rarely remains at that level. Reporting their own experiences Born and Sawyer (1979) have this to say:

the time-contracting method does help control the flood of referrals, and by maintaining this control, enables the psychologist to pursue other areas of work of equal importance. The concentration on time for a school gives more opportunity for intervention within the school system, rather than only with the individual child. This enables other time to be free for research, study, work in units, and preventive measures.

Born and Sawyer make it clear that this basic arrangement for disposing their work-time provides a starting point only—a point from which casework with individuals can be extended into a more comprehensive form of intervention. The priority for psychologists is to develop the skills and ways of thinking appropriate to the levels of action that are evidently necessary.

The concept of the *system* embodied in general systems theory provides a possible framework for thinking more adequately about problem behaviour in schools, mainly because of its implications for the kind of action we should take (see Chapter 2). Systems theory at first, or even second, take has something of an alien and rather abstract feel about it. It may also seem, at one level, over-simple and over-general, but this is also to be seen as characteristic of its wide range of reference and manageability in use. In considering the psychology of problem behaviour the idea of human beings and social institutions as systems enables us to get out of the conceptual straightjacket of traditional cause-effect psychology—e.g. that a child's problems are caused by his home background or his low intelligence, or even his 'maladjustment'.

'A system,' write Kast and Rosenzweig (1976), 'is an organised or complex whole: an assemblage or combination of things or parts forming a complete or unitary whole.' Human and social systems are but two levels of this concept of complex assemblies of elements, which do not 'cause' each other but mutually interact and affect each other. Thus to change any element is to change the whole system to a greater or lesser degree. The 'change-value' of a single element is not absolute but relative to the other parts of the whole—hence the inadequacy or unpredictability of main-cause to main-effect explanations and actions. As a corollary (see Chapters 3 and 4) there are no simple defining features of successful or unsuccessful schools: this implies caution in attempting any literal translation of the characteristics of the one to the other. Similarly a beneficial modification in one school (like the timetabling changes described in Chapter 8) will not necessarily have the same outcome in another school. Because of this, and because behaviour is usually multiply determined, system change requires careful evaluation of probable effects (and therefore careful *planning*) and action at several levels more or less simultaneously, in particular the individual as well as the institutional level.

If psychology is concerned with the behaviour and emotions of individuals it follows that an adequate concept of the psychological system of an individual has to include the settings and tasks and relationships within which the individual feels and behaves. Changes in a person's knowledge or understanding, in his relationships or situation, all introduce new elements which are not just added or substituted, but rather result in a different interaction between the various elements of his personal system – a different whole individual.

This comparatively simple suggestion has important implications for theory and practice. In particular, it implies that change for an individual may need to be at several levels and related to both internal and external elements in his 'system'. Thus we *may* be able to change a child's behaviour by working with him directly to alter his attitudes or improve his social skills, i.e. 'treating' the individual (although the evidence is against the general effectiveness of this in isolation); or we may be able to change him (his system) by altering, for example, the physical setting within which he operates (e.g. in one classroom instead of half a dozen); the tasks he has to fulfil (e.g. replanning the curriculum he has to cope with); the functions of his role (e.g. simplifying school rules to a clearly specified and well-policed minimum); the relationship demands he encounters (e.g. modification of teacher-handling of classroom situations, separating older and younger children at breaktimes by timetabling changes). (Chapters 8 and 9 describe this approach in practice.) Changing these 'external' elements in the child's psychological system is, of course, also to change some aspects of the social system of the school *with which the child's own system interacts.*

It would be absurd, as well as impossible, for a school system – cumbersome and multi-purpose as it is – to make frequent and unique adaptations to individuals. But such adaptations are rarely unique: the problems posed by the vulnerable child (to use a charitable term) indicate changes that may well improve the functioning of the school for many more children who do not present overt problems. This is a point better recognised in preventive medicine: a physical environment that predisposes respiratory disorders in a delicate minority is unlikely to be satisfactory even for the majority who are not so vulnerable. Having said that, the best conceivable environment will still have its 'unhealthy' residue. There will always be a number of children who

cannot be helped or accommodated in the best feasible school organisation; the danger lies in assuming prematurely that such a state has
been achieved. Individuals vary in their physical and psychological
thresholds. Because only a minority of children present behaviour
problems in school it does not follow that the school is not a key
factor in the problem, and only changes in some aspect of the school's
organisation and practice will reveal this.

But why should schools have to change? Why should they bear the
brunt of falling standards, of a more permissive society, of the influence
of the media, etc., etc? These familiar rhetorical questions are not meant
to dismiss the argument; clearly there has been a progressive slackening
of social inhibitions especially in relation to violent and aggressive
behaviour. It is difficult to specify how this has come about, let alone
how the trend can be reversed. Schools interact with the wider institutions
of society and cannot escape from that: at the same time they are not
passive victims and any influence is bound to be two-way. Furthermore,
it is not just 'society' that has been changing, but schools as well. It is
likely that the difficulties experienced in managing learning failure and
problem behaviour have been created to some extent by the great
changes that have taken place in secondary school organisation during
the past twenty years. This is no judgement on comprehensive schools
as such, but it is a necessary and valid comment to point out that such
schools are typically much more complicated institutions than anything
we have had before; and complex systems have problems and characteristics of their own. The complexity is not simply in terms of *size*, but
also in the range of *functions* that are now considered appropriate to a
school and in the scope of the *curriculum*. Even the complexity
introduced by a wider social class mix, or by co-education of the sexes,
add dimensions to the organisation — with an exponential increase in
the interactive relationships between the elements in the system. That
problems of communication are often apparently endemic in some
secondary schools is not surprising. Such problems can be solved and
are, indeed, dealt with routinely in much larger commercial institutions,
but the process has to become deliberate and formalised; it cannot
occur 'naturally'. The traditional informal scrutiny of senior staff
appropriate to medium-sized secondary schools of a restricted function
is insufficient in our larger, more complex comprehensives. The watchful
eye of the first lieutenant is not enough: something akin to a research
strategy is required.

   This style of investigation is one that psychologists have some
experience of during their undergraduate studies but more rarely in

their post-graduate training in educational psychology. The latter is still usually preoccupied with the individual assessment and diagnosis of children. To be useful in our large secondary schools the psychologist needs to be not clinician/diagnostician so much as advisory colleague/researcher. And he needs to be *in* the schools, familiar to all members of staff. Tizard's (1973) more than half-serious suggestion that educational psychologists should be based in schools from where they could get in touch with their clinics by telephone, points the required emphasis. Whether working at the level of the individual 'case' or at what is already perceived as a more general problem, knowledge of the school and the people in it is indispensable to explanation and action. The educational psychologist is well placed to take this individual-to-institutional perspective: on the one hand, working at the level of what school means for a particular child in difficulty; on the other, analysing situations which predispose behaviour problems in general. The information and insights gained have then to be made available to individual tutors and those responsible for day-to-day management so as to provide a rational basis for change or development. Such a process need not detract from the traditional autonomy enjoyed by schools or teachers since the responsibility for action is theirs. Discussing this sort of approach in relation to truancy, Gregory (1980) suggests that 'such action research *should be part of a school's on-going activity*' (my italics) — in other words, not just open-and-shut research projects but a continuous process of investigation at various problem levels. It is a form of influence with long-term, preventive implications.

A 'systems' approach is not a synonym for an organisational approach, nor does it imply that all behaviour problems will disappear simply as a consequence of manipulating institutional processes. Rather, it is a productive way of thinking about social problems in school in that it forces consideration of what have been the missing elements in an adequate psychology of individuals — which may lead to investigation of other, intersecting, systems whether individual or institutional. It does not involve a neglect of individuals: our conception of the individual has been too narrow. The social psychologist, Geoffrey Stephenson (1981) summarises the argument:

> It is high time that psychologists stopped offering individual characteristics as an explanation of social behaviour and as a solution to social problems. To change behaviour we must discover what in the institutional arrangements is supporting the behaviour that we want changed. We must discover what it is within the prescribed

relationships that is engendering the behaviour in question . . . (p. 448)

Acknowledgement

I am indebted to Robert Daines, Martin Desforges and Janet Ouston who read a late draft of this chapter, making many helpful comments and suggestions.

2 SYSTEMS THEORY AND ITS RELEVANCE TO SCHOOLS

Robert Burden

The purpose of this chapter is to provide an introduction to some ways in which systems theory can offer an approach to understanding behaviour problems in schools. The task is a difficult one since it involves drawing together ideas from different branches of psychology and sociology and to a certain extent reformulating these within the context of education. However, it seems important at this level to opt for clarity at the risk of some over-simplification. Those wishing to delve deeper into the theoretical issues involved will be referred to appropriate texts where necessary.

There can be no doubt that behaviour problems in schools are currently a major cause for concern amongst the teaching profession. The fact that this has probably always been the case is of less interest to us here than the explanations that have been given to account for such problems. An excellent discussion of this area is provided by Haigh (1976), who highlights the point that the way in which people suggest that disruptive or problem pupils should be dealt with illustrates their underlying assumptions about the aetiology of the problem. A good example of this is his observation (p. 115) that suspension or exclusion from classes within school of pupils classified as difficult or disruptive, can only be contemplated by a teaching profession which has decided that the problems of schools are largely the result of pressures from outside.

There is a sense in which such an assumption can be seen as part of a continuum in the development of theories and methodological approaches to deviance (Buckley 1967). At the one end are causal theories of the 'bad seed' type, in which the source of all the problems is seen as lying within the individual from the start, apparently inherited or due to immutable early experiences. At the other extreme the onus of blame is laid entirely on forces within the environment, with a more sophisticated version in between suggesting a complex interaction of hereditary and environmental forces. Traditionally, psychologists have been viewed as more concerned with the first kind of explanation whilst sociologists were seen to be totally concerned with the wider environment in their search for the roots of deviance. Thus, one could contrast the approaches of, say, Eysenck (1964) and Merton (1957) in their efforts to account for criminal behaviour. However, in an attempt to specify more precisely the important variables affecting the interaction of individuals within specific environments, some sociologists and social psychologists began to concern themselves with more immediate events at the micro-level of social transactions. The most influential psychologist in this area has undoubtedly been George Kelly, and amongst sociologists the views of the so-called 'labelling theorists' have received a great deal of attention (see Hargreaves 1978b).

Buckley (1967) suggests that it was in an attempt to bridge the gap between the latter view of deviant behaviour as having been transactionally generated and the wider structural normative background from which it emerged, that sociologists first became interested in the conceptual possibilities offered by the newly developing science of cybernetics and the notion of the feedback loop. It is one short step from here to conceptualising deviance as a product of forces within systems generated out of a network of ongoing events or processes. The educational psychologist might well argue that an important missing component within such a sociological viewpoint is the individual and what he or she brings to the various interactions as a result of his genetic endowment and early experiences, but this need not concern us for the moment — especially as it is not necessarily true. What the sociological perspective does enable us to do is to move on to consider a number of aspects of behavioural deviance that might otherwise be overlooked by psychologists. First, there is a movement away from the kind of theory that seeks to explain behaviour in terms of inputs and outputs and a movement towards the need to consider the processes by which social activities are performed. (See Cohen (1965) for an eloquent summary of this aspect of deviance theory.) Secondly, at least one sociologist, Erving Goffman (1961), has been led to consider ways in which large institutions such as prisons and mental hospitals affect the lives of their inmates by the very nature of their organisational structure. This pioneer work of Goffman can be seen as the direct precursor of such important educational studies as those of Partridge (1966), Hargreaves (1967) and Lacey (1970).

Buckley suggests that the study of the history of scientific thinking over the past few centuries can help us to understand the development of systems theory. He sees the latter as a product of a constant dialectic between conceptions of physical and biological science during which there has been a movement away from concern for inherent substance, qualities and properties towards a greater interest in the principles of organisation *per se*, regardless of what it is that is organised. This, in turn, led to the realisation by such scientific philosophers as Whitehead that the procedures and concepts of biology, particularly in the emphasis placed upon teleological (or purposive) explanations and on classification and categorisation, offered a more helpful approach to the problems of organisational complexity than did the traditional procedures of physics. Rapopart and Horvarth (1959) have suggested that the important link between the general approach of biological holism and the development of specific theoretical structures and methods of the systems approach arose out of these biological concepts of teleology and taxonomy of 'purposes' and classifications. Thus teleology became incorporated into the ideas of cybernetics and was made 'respectable' by the application of physical laws and principles to the construction of networks of causal relations, including the idea of the closed-loop feedback. In this way it became possible to define goal-seeking behaviour operationally without resorting to traditional teleological explanations. Secondly, but perhaps less pertinent to the present discussion, is the suggestion that the taxonomic function is best fulfilled by the sort of plan which employs descriptive, or qualitative, rather than quantitative terms.

At this point we should be nearer to some kind of explanation as to what is meant by a system (in the sociological sense) and to outlining the conceptual requirements necessary to enable us to study its effects.

We can consider a system as comprising a number of components directly or indirectly related in a causal network, such that each component is related to at least some others in a more or less stable way within any particular period of time. These components are by no means necessarily static entities. They can be roles or procedures or even hypothetical structures. Thus, in the case of a school, some of the components might well be the roles allocated to various members of staff, the departmental structure, the streaming or banding procedure, the disciplinary regulations and organisation of pastoral care. Such components may be relatively simple and stable or complex and changing. They will also vary in their interrelations, sometimes mutual, sometimes unidirectional or intermittent, but almost always arranged within some form of overt or covert hierarchy.

It will inevitably happen that certain of the components or elements of any system will become established in a more or less stable set of relationships in such a way as to produce a sense of 'wholeness' with

some degree of continuity and boundary. Thus the systemic concept
of a school goes far beyond the actual visibly structured components
of buildings, books, people, etc., to incorporate elements of the kind
outlined above *and the relationships between those elements.* It can go
even further if we accept the view of Ashby (1956) that an open system
is constantly in a dynamic state of change so that over time it becomes
more characterised by the experiences that have occurred within it than
by its initial state. This cybernetic viewpoint of Ashby's is important
for our consideration of possible applications of systems theory to
schools in that it re-emphasises the need to consider *process* variables
as well as those of input and product (see also Stufflebeam 1969). If
we are too simplistic in our application of systems analysis, for example,
we may well find that by metaphorically taking a system to pieces we
would be unable to reassemble it since we would be left with a vast
number of separate parts or items of information without understanding
the relationship between them.

We can now begin to formulate several possible advantages of a
systems approach to deviance or behaviour problems in schools.

(1) It offers a framework within which we can consider large
    complex organisations such as comprehensive schools and
    the ways in which they function.

(2) It makes clear that a piecemeal approach centred on problems
    is nonsensical when seen within the framework of such
    organisational complexity, since the intricate relationship of
    parts cannot be treated out of context of the whole.

(3) It emphasises the need to study *relations* rather than entities,
    with process and change variables considered to be of vital
    importance.

(4) It offers far greater opportunities for realistic change than any
    other intervention model since it suggests not only that
    behaviour described as deviant can be understood within any
    specific context, but also that various behavioural outcomes
    can be predicted as a result of a well-designed systems analysis
    and systems change.

There is a need at this stage to emphasise that what has been outlined
is by no means the only available description of 'a systems approach'.
Dale (1972) suggests that there are at least five major approaches to the
study of organisations, each of which has a different theoretical orientation and tends to conceptualise systems and their problems in a

basically different way. It is perhaps hardly surprising that this should
be the case when we realise that each has been developed within a
different frame of reference. Thus, the *human relations* approach has
its roots in social psychology, tends to consider organisations in a vacuum
and centres upon ways of achieving satisfaction within the work group
in order to attain managerial goals. The approach of *organisational
psychology*, on the other hand, concentrates more upon the problem
of achieving compatibility between the needs of the individual personality and of the system, which in itself is seen as being affected by the
personality dimension. The concept of 'self-actualisation' is central to
this approach.

The description given so far in this chapter can probably best be
seen as an amalgam of two other approaches: *structural functionalism*
with its roots in sociology, and the other, usually referred to as *decision-
making theory*, which derives from economics and cybernetics. The
former views the environment as a source of problems and concentrates
upon the nature of the interdependence of social systems and the ways
in which they adjust their dynamic equilibrium in response to threats
to their survival. The fourth approach, decision-making theory, is more
concerned with the nature of the decision-making process in relation
to the stability and growth of organisations particularly where these are
affected by restrictions within the environment.

The fifth approach is one which has had considerable influence upon
some educators and is perhaps worth describing in greater detail. This
is usually referred to as the *socio-technical systems* approach and is
epitomised in a large body of work emanating from the Tavistock
Institute for Human Relations under the auspices of A.K. Rice and
E.J. Miller (Rice 1963; Miller & Rice 1967). A central concept of this
approach, which appears to stem from an amalgam of psychology and
economics, is that of the 'primary task'. Every organisation is seen as
having a primary task that it must perform in order to survive and this
is achieved by means of an 'import-conversion-export' paradigm. At
its simplest level, the primary task of a school could be seen as importing
children and converting them into educated young people ready to take
their place in an adult world at the time of their export.

One helpful aspect of this approach is that it brings us face to face
with the question of what sort of business schools see themselves as
being in, i.e. what do they see themselves as preparing their pupils for
and how are they intending to accomplish this? As Richardson (1973)
points out in her influential study of Nailsea Comprehensive School
based on this approach, once we begin to look closely at the primary

task of a complex institution such as a school, we find a number of conflicting interests emerging. Richardson draws upon an early conceptualisation of Miller that institutions may be divided along the dimensions of territory, time and technology, to suggest that schools can be construed in a similar way. Thus, the *territory* dimension involves the curriculum as well as more structural entities such as form rooms, house bases or sixth-form blocks; *time* is involved in the timetabling of lessons, the differentiation between 'work' and 'leisure' or 'in-school' and 'out-of-school' activities, etc; *technology* comes into play in both the range of subjects offered to pupils and the ways in which these are taught. The main point here is that there are bound to be discontinuities and even conflicts arising between these 'second-order systems'. The task of a consultant, in Richardson's terms, would be to clarify where such discontinuities are occurring and to help the school to find ways of managing, but not necessarily eliminating, them in such a way that pupils can be helped to cope with them.

It is necessary to emphasise at this juncture an important point made by Dale (1972) that none of these approaches can offer a general theory of organisations. In fact, he goes on to wonder whether any theory of organisations could be anything more than partial. All that each of these theories can do is to offer an approach to understanding and changing some aspects of what is happening within one or another type of organisation. It seems likely that education could stand to benefit from the application of each of them at one point or another, but as yet we are a long way from such an integrated approach.

Before turning from the more sociological view of systems and organisational theory, it would perhaps be as well to comment upon one or two British educational sociologists who have written persuasively in this area. A simple sociological introduction to the school as an organisation is given by Musgrave (1968); a more sophisticated but readable text on a similar theme is that of Shipman (1968). Lambert *et al.* (1970) offer a useful manual incorporating methods and techniques for assessing the goals and the formal and the informal social order operating within schools.

As is often the case in the history of science, the development of ideas about the ways in which systems operate seems to have occurred more or less concurrently within more than one branch of science. The biologist Ludwig von Bertalanffy is usually acknowledged as being the first to use the term 'general systems theory' and to set out an original set of

basic concepts about its application (see Kast and Rosenweig 1976).
This was then taken up largely in the United States both within the
physical and biological sciences and within industry.

One of the most important contributions of von Bertalanffy was the
concept of the 'open' as opposed to the 'closed' system. A closed
system is one which is considered in isolation and therefore assumed
to be self-contained. As such it has the inherent characteristic of
moving first towards 'static equilibrium' and finally towards 'entropy
of random chaos' – to use the language of cybernetics and thermo-
dynamics. When organisations are looked upon as closed systems the
emphasis is always upon internal structure, tasks and formal relationships
considered in isolation without reference to external environment. An
open system, on the other hand, is one which cannot be considered
outside its relationships with the environment in which it exists. It can
only continue to function as a result of a dynamic two-way relationship
with the environment and thereby avoids the danger of entropy that
constantly threatens closed systems. This leads to the concept of 'steady
state', the dynamic equilibrium achieved by the successful open system
by means of continual feedback with the environment. Here we begin
to see the influence of cybernetics.

There are several other important characteristics of organisational
systems. In order to maintain balance and equilibrium a system must
develop mechanisms that maintain the status quo but also keep the
system sensitive to the need for change. As these become more effective,
'boundaries' will be set up that make it possible to differentiate a
contrived – as opposed to a 'natural' – system from its environment.
Growth will take place by means of a process of internal elaboration
whereby a more complex structure of management and organisation
will evolve.

Kast and Rosenzweig (1976) highlight three levels of management
within organisations that can be seen to overlap with those suggested
by Richardson (1973). Here a distinction is drawn between the *technical*
level which is concerned with actual task performance, the *institutional*
level which relates the activities of the system to its environment, and
the *organisational* level where the task is to integrate the technical level
with the institutional level. There is a danger that in concentrating upon
just the technical level, managers will take a closed-system view that
must inevitably lead to decay. On the other hand, management just
at an institutional level could lapse into mere rhetoric or pious hopes
unless appropriate action is taken at the technical level to ensure that
goals are achieved. Thus, in facing situations that are by the very nature

of open systems, dynamic, inherently uncertain and frequently
ambiguous, managers must develop skills at all three levels or arrange
situations that enable them to be established within the organisation
itself.

But what can we draw from this mass of rather abstract information,
derived from widely differing disciplines, that can be of value in considering behaviour problems in schools? What follows must inevitably
be a personal view of some of the more interesting implications for
senior staff in schools, educational psychologists and the like. First, it
goes without saying that problems must be viewed in the widest possible
context. This is not to suggest that they will always be entirely environ-
mentally based nor that the interactionist view of deviance as described
by the labelling theorists can possibly provide a totally satisfactory
explanation of all disruptive behaviour in schools. What it does mean is
that we can start at the institutional level and work from the supposition
that many examples of behaviour described as disruptive or problem-
atical by those working within a position of authority in schools can
be viewed as problems of the schools themselves rather than of
individuals or 'society'.

The necessary approach for working within the framework of systems
theory is to start from the assumption that schools exist and that
children must attend them and will be expected to act in certain ways
when they do. Such an approach does not dispute that some problems
may well stem from within an individual child or from within an
individual teacher, but seeks to understand how the explicit and
implicit organisational structure of a school affects the perceptions and
behaviour of its pupils in a way that leads them to be seen as problem-
atical or disruptive by those faced with the task of maintaining that
structure. Structure here is used in the broad sense described above rather
than in its traditionally more formal sense.

The school needs to be seen as an open system in constant dynamic
interaction with the environment that it serves, both in regard to the
local neighbourhood or town and to the current expectations or
demands of society at large. Its success will be viewed according to
how well it maintains an internal state of equilibrium whilst adapting
to the ever-changing needs of society and therefore of its (the school's)
products. The success with which the school defines its primary task (its
aims) and manages by various human and technological means to
accomplish its objectives, will have a vitally important bearing on the

sense of satisfaction achieved by its inmates – both at a teaching and learning level. Skemp (1979) has argued that the very nature of the role-demands made upon the various participants within schools must inevitably lead to conflict, but this is not a view that the systems analyst would share. Systems theory argues that dynamic tension is a potentially positive rather than negative sign, provided that the necessary feedback mechanisms are operating effectively within the system in order to implement a required balancing-out effect.

The major issue with which we are now faced is not concerned with the why or how of systems theory. I have argued elsewhere (Burden 1978; 1979a, 1979b) that there is an increasing fund of information that can be used in carrying out successful school-based systems analysis. What we need now is more practical experience in doing it. The exciting prospect facing us is whether we can progress to a more effective systems design which would mean more effective schools for the children and adults who work in them – and a more satisfactory outcome for society as a whole.

3 THE EFFECTS OF SCHOOL: A RADICAL FAITH RE-STATED

David Reynolds and Michael Sullivan

I

For those who believe that the educational system in general and individual schools in particular can do little to ameliorate the adolescent and adult problems of the society around them, the experiences and evidence of the last decade have apparently provided much evidence to confirm them in their belief. Both Third World and developed countries alike have discovered that increased educational expenditures do not necessarily lead to an increase in levels of economic growth and wealth production. Developed societies – like the United States and Britain – that have also been pursuing policies of educational expansion in the hope of generating greater equality of opportunity amongst different social groups, have further discovered the difficulty of attaining these desirable social goals merely by means of 'social engineering' via the formal educational system. General changes in the organisation of systems of secondary schooling (as in Britain), specific programmes of individual school reform and school change, programmes of specific curriculum modification and further programmes of compensatory education have all been found – in Britain and the United States, at least – to be relatively ineffective and unsuccessful in changing any of the pupil characteristics that reformers have wished to affect. Furthermore, the substantial body of research knowledge that has accumulated in the last fifteen years from sources as varied as the British Plowden Report *Children and their Primary Schools* (Central Advisory Council for Education 1967), the American Coleman Report *Equality of Educational Opportunity* (Coleman 1966) and the reviews of both British and American research literature reported in Christopher Jencks' much publicised study *Inequality* (Jencks *et al.* 1972) have appeared to show a quite consistent message: that what a child takes from his or her school depends very little upon the quality of the school experience itself but very greatly on the nature of the pupil's intelligence and family and community background.

Schools have been widely regarded by educational researchers and by others as making no difference to anything of importance. Educational services have become, as Wilby (1977) labels them, the *Titanic* of the state welfare systems. Educational reform, to use Wilby again, is increasingly regarded as equivalent in importance to rearranging the furniture on the great ship's maiden voyage.

In this chapter we wish to re-affirm the conventional radical faith which sees schooling as an important determinant of the nature of adolescent and adult society, social problems and social patterns. We shall review and critically evaluate the evidence, both negative and positive, as to the effectiveness of educational expansion, change in school system organisation, the introduction of innovations and the use of compensatory education in attaining academic and social goals. And we shall conclude — echoing the old, radical faith — that the school itself may be able to combat adolescent problems by means of processes that involve institutional change and modification. Detailed discussion of the ways in which this may be achieved are to be found in Chapter 4 and succeeding chapters.

The Liberal Dream

The enthusiasm of Government and society at large for the educational reform and expansion of the 1960s in Britain and the United States was, of course, no novel cultural phenomenon. Commitment to expanded and reformed 'education' as a means of ensuring social reform, ameliorating social problems and encouraging a development of talent that would benefit both individuals and the society around them, has been a characteristic feature of the ideology of radical members of the British upper class and of radical or socialist politicians since the beginning of the Victorian age. As Ferge (1977) notes, at least three factors contributed to this faith in education at the time of the Industrial Revolution:

> The first was the humanistic perspective connected with the Enlightenment, that held cultural values in special esteem and wanted to make them available to the biggest number possible. The second was the realisation that the new class differences based on new objective conditions required a new ideology and new methods of transmitting it in order to make it acceptable . . . The third factor was connected with the effective requirements of production: the new techniques that had to be applied in the division of labour could be acquired less and less as part of the normal socialisation process within the family because of two interconnected reasons: quick technical change and

a high rate of occupational mobility. (p. 13)

Governmental desire to enlighten populations in traditional Christian morality, to ensure their social and political compliance and the continuing 'need' to train populations in constantly changing skills, provide, then, predisposing factors that would probably have prompted some form of educational change in any decade. The precipitating factors that brought about the massive social experiments in education that characterised the 1960s are, however, in many ways peculiar to that period. Such factors were the declining potency and force of the church and family as agents of normal suasion and the growing research evidence of the ineffectiveness of conventional and curative measures like social-work intervention and approved-school placement in dealing with the social problems of youth. The research evidence that linked failure at school with a wide variety of adolescent problems such as truancy, delinquency, vandalism, psychiatric disorder and alcohol abuse, also made educational reform and expansion an attractive policy option (for further discussion, see Reynolds and Jones 1978).

However, it is clear that the principal factor that precipitated the educational reform and expansion of the 1960s was the nature of the programmes and general policy orientation of the British Labour Party. To a party wanting to change society peacefully and without the required major structural changes in the ownership of the means of production, social change through the proxy of the educational system was an attractive option, since it

> was more politically palatable and less socially disruptive than direct measures of tackling inequality. . . . Ugly words such as redistribution and expropriation did not apply in education, or nobody thought they applied. Education was a cornucopia so prolific of good things that nobody would need any longer to ask awkward questions about who got what. (Wilby 1977, p. 358)

The Labour Party, although it had flirted with an 'institutional redistributive' model of the Welfare State after the Second World War when its aims had been those socialist principles of equality, humanitarianism and social fellowship, had moved to a more conservative view of the Welfare State and its goals by the early 1960s. By the time of the 1964 General Election, educational reform was merely to accomplish three things:

(i)   The generation of more highly qualified talent which would in turn generate more wealth both for the talented and for the collectivity.

(ii)   The generation of greater equality of opportunity for those social groups formerly deprived or disadvantaged from the possession of educational qualifications.

(iii) The successful combating of adolescent social problems that were regarded as having their roots in part in failure at school.

The first aim of educational reform reflected the revival in influence of the human-capital school of economic theorists. Although the theory can be seen as dating from the writings of Adam Smith, the popularity of these ideas in the 1960s owes much to Theodore W. Shultz, an American economist who argued that education should be seen as a form of *investment*, rather than a form of personal consumption, since 'by investing in themselves people can enlarge the range of choices open to them' (Shultz, quoted in Bernbaum 1979, p. 8). Both the Robbins Report and the Newsom Report of 1963 on the education of the child of average and less than average ability reflected this philosophy, with the latter arguing that 'there is much unrealised talent especially amongst boys and girls whose potential is marred by inadequate powers of speech and the limitations of home background . . . the country cannot afford this wastage, humanly or economically speaking' (Central Advisory Council for Education 1963, para 3); whilst the former report argued that increased investment in facilities for higher education would have economic and social benefits for the population as a whole (Committee on Higher Education 1963).

   The second aim of educational reform – the amelioration and long-term removal of *inequalities of opportunity* as between different social class groups – had been a consistent theme in the policy of the Labour Party of the early 1960s. Anthony Crosland spoke for many social democrats in the party when he argued that there was 'an irresistible pressure in British society to extend rights of citizenship' (Crosland 1974). The research evidence showing consistent inequalities between social classes and racial groups in their educational opportunity (Douglas 1968) was interpreted as showing the influence of factors in the pupils' homes (such as material disadvantage or social deprivation), but also as reflecting on the nature of the bi-partite system of grammar and secondary modern schools, which 'reinforced' or 'intensified' pre-existing differences between different pupil groups.

   As well as ensuring the promotion of social justice and of equality of opportunity (with a consequent reduction in social-class antagonism), educational reform was hoped by many in the early 1960s to be capable of ensuring a *reduction in adolescent deviance* both within and without the schools. In a strikingly similar way to the influence exerted by the 'blocked-goal attainment' hypotheses of Albert Cohen (1955) and Richard Cloward (1961) upon the American Democratic Party Government's 'War on Poverty' that was launched in 1963, British research evidence of the same period consistently linked failure at school with delinquency outside. Whilst 'home factors' were usually held to be in part responsible for such deviance, many radicals and liberals argued — like the Longford Study Group Report of 1966 — that:

> Anti-social behaviour in the child may arise from difficulties at home, *from unhappiness at school,* from physical or mental handicap or maladjustment, or from a variety of other causes, for which the child has no personal responsibility. (quoted in Clarke 1980)

School reform was, it was hoped, a factor that would succeed in curbing the tendencies of potentially troublesome adolescent youth.

The Shattering of the Liberal Dream

The predisposing and precipitating factors that we have mentioned above led directly to a large variety of educational policies and reforms that were pursued in the latter part of the 1960s. In 1965, the Circular 10/65 was issued by the Labour Government which requested local authorities to submit plans for the reorganisation of their secondary schools upon comprehensive lines. Following on from the Plowden Report of 1967, positive discrimination in favour of schools of certain socially deprived areas was introduced in a limited attempt to promote equality of opportunity for children living in these areas. Gross expenditure on education increased from £1,768 million in 1966 to £6,840 million in 1975, which represented an increase of from 5.28 per cent to 7.27 per cent of Gross National Product. The school leaving age, which was to have been raised to 16 by the Labour Government in 1964/70, was finally raised by the Conservatives in 1973. Expansion of nursery school education proposed in the White Paper *Education for Expansion* (DES 1972) would, it was hoped, release women for work and tackle the roots of social and educational deprivation that were believed to take effect before formal schooling began.

As well as an increase in the quantity of the education given to each child and a change in the nature of secondary, primary and pre-school organisation, the years 1965 to 1975 saw a plethora of educational innovations. Some were concerned with curriculum change, some also involved changes in teaching methods; some involved the deployment of greater quantities of educational technology and teaching aids and others involved programmes of planned change in schools, utilising a large battery of methods and means. Other innovations included the development of various strategies of compensatory education, programmes which were much employed in the United States (for detailed evidence see Whiteside 1978, Schools Council 1973, Stenhouse 1980).

These many and varied educational policies are now widely argued as having failed to attain their goals. Bernbaum (1979) talks of 'the inefficacy of remedy', politicians increasingly that 'school doesn't matter' (quoted in Hodgson 1973) and also increasingly, academic discussions of the causes of pupil failure and pupil problems have reverted to explanations that look to genetic factors (Jensen 1971), environmental factors (Davie *et al.* 1972) and/or the macrostructure of capitalist society (Bowles and Gintis 1976) for their causal explanations. The school is — to adopt the title of Husen's (1979) book on this same theme — increasingly in question.

It is important to realise, though, that much of the evidence assembled in the 1970s, which has been used in attempts to discount the possibilities of attaining social change by means of educational change, is itself open to a variety of interpretations. The failure of educational reform to generate more wealth in both developed and underdeveloped countries (see Husen 1979, Ch. 2) may well be due to a variety of factors, such as the onset of the economic crisis that occurred after the expansion of educational expenditures. Much of the extra manpower generated from secondary or higher education was, in any case, not of direct and immediate use for the generation of wealth. Educational expansion *per se* may not be ineffective — only a certain qualitative variety of expansion.

It could be argued in a similar vein that the continuing substantial inequalities between social classes in their educational attainments at primary school (Davie *et al.* 1972), upon leaving school (Douglas 1968) or in their access to higher education (Westergaard and Reisler 1975) , may merely reflect the continuing large inequalities in the allocation of educational resources between lower social class and higher social class regions (Byrne and Williamson 1975) and between different residential areas within such regions (Tunley 1979). The lessons of the years of increased expenditure may be that expansion of educational resources that maintains pre-existing inequalities in resource allocation may not have any effect in reducing societal inequalities. Whether expansion of the educational system accompanied by redistribution would be more effective is unknown.

Also, it is possible that the apparent lack of effectiveness of comprehensive school reform in attaining any of the goals of its proponents (Ford 1969; Steedman 1980) may merely reflect the fact that the comprehensive schools are simply re-creating under one roof the institutions of selection that were previously to be found under different institutional arrangements (see Benn and Simon 1970 for an indication of this, and Reynolds and Sullivan 1979 for further evidence). Comprehensive schools may make no difference, then, because they represent no difference in the quality of education consumed by most pupils. It may well be that the lack of effectiveness of many of the school-based curriculum innovations may reflect upon the poor forward planning prior to their introduction, the inadequate training of those teachers involved, the lack of monitoring or feedback to participating institutions and the frequently unclear formulations of goals evident in many of the projects. The failures of attempts to 'start pupils early' on French in the primary school, for example, could be due to negative teacher attitudes towards teaching the subject to those groups (Burstall 1970). The failure of language labs likewise may be a function of their abuse or mis-use (Wilby 1977).

Many possible conclusions from the evidence about the failure of educational reform are possible, then, other than the widely accepted conclusion that education *cannot* compensate for, or affect, the nature of the pupils or the wider society. Certainly, many educational policies did not attain their goals but this may simply indicate the lack of difference that the policies made to the practice of education they were meant to affect. Many of the policy changes were more apparent than real, as is likely to be the case with many of the changes in the nature of secondary school organisation, curriculum reform and teaching methods. The question of the lack of potency of the system to fulfil the hopes of social reformers may well be a somewhat less settled issue than many accounts have hitherto suggested to us. Educational reform of a substantive kind may still have a potency that minor and trivial changes in educational policy have hidden.

Do Schools Make No Difference?

The apparent failure of educational social engineering has had a profound effect on professional, governmental and public opinion, diluting the liberal idealism and expectations of the 1960s. One of the most important factors in this process has been the accumulation of evidence which suggested that differences between schools have only quite minimal effects upon their pupils and that, therefore, the individual school is not a strong determinant of the nature of children entering the wider society. The research evidence upon which these claims have been made – and we shall see that this evidence is not really capable of supporting the definitive conclusions that have been widely drawn from it – is mostly American, although some contribution to the debate has been made from British sources.

The American debate on this issue was largely begun by the Coleman Report, entitled *Equality of Educational Opportunity*, which was published in 1966. Data collected from over 600,000 children, from 60,000 teachers and from 4,000 schools showed, when analysed by means of multiple regression analysis, that there were substantial differences between the verbal ability levels of the children from various minority races and those the report called 'white' children. Whilst the differences between these groups of children were substantially greater upon leaving school than on entering it, the report argued that these apparent effects of schools upon pupils' attainments were merely a reflection of the social composition of the pupil body in the schools that the children of different races attended at that time and were not a reflection of the quality of the schools themselves. When all things were equal, such factors as the amount of money spent on each pupil, the number of books in the school library, the quality of the schools' physical and recreational resources and even differences in the nature of the schools' curricula seemed to make little appreciable difference to minority group or white children's levels of attainment on verbal ability tests.

The data collected for the Coleman Report and other longitudinal data upon pupils, schools, school districts and communities were re-analysed by Christopher Jencks and his colleagues and published in 1972 under the title *Inequality*. In most respects, the results of this second major study parallel those of the first. As with the Coleman Report, measures of school resources are shown to be a very poor predictor of student performance – a much higher proportion of variance between individuals in their ability scores is explicable by knowledge of the socio-economic status of the individual's parents and of the intelligence quotient of that individual, rather than by the physical or social quality of the schools that the individual might attend. Jencks attempted to quantify precisely how much variation in attainment is attributable to school resources and concluded very pessimistically that, 'Qualitative differences between high schools seem to explain about 2 per cent of the variation in students' educational attainment' (Jencks 1972, p. 159).

These findings which suggested that school characteristics have relatively little effect upon student attainment or student performance have been replicated in a veritable host of studies published in the United States from the late 1960s to the mid-1970s. Work by the economist Hanushek (1972), for example, shows no relationship between school resources and student performance on test scores. The small relationship he found between test scores and the verbal ability of teachers hardly suggests, as Hurn (1978) notes, an easy strategy that would narrow the differences in achievement between students from different social origins. The review of a further 21 studies by authors working for the Rand Corporation (Averch *et al.* 1971) concludes un-equivocally that, 'Research has not identified a variant of the existing system that is consistently related to students' educational outcomes' (p. 171). A review of the literature by Stephens (1967) also suggests that, contrary to the opinion of many educationalists, there is no clear evidence that any factors such as pupil/teacher ratios, different teaching styles and different curriculum patterns have a consistent relationship with differences in student ability.

The findings of the American research on the effects of schools were, then, apparently clear cut. Combined with similar results from detailed analyses of the influence of home and school factors in the Plowden Report (Peaker 1967) and set alongside the continuing tendency of British researchers to concentrate upon detailed analysis only of the influence of family and community factors that might affect pupil development – as exemplified by studies such as *From Birth to Seven* that have emanated from the National Children's Bureau – the result was substantially to erode any belief in the effectiveness of schooling, (a) amongst the academic community undertaking educational research, (b) amongst politicians (particularly in the United States) and (c) amongst teachers exposed to simplistic portrayals of the findings of the research by the popular media.

II

Schools May Make a Difference

During the last ten years or so a number of factors have combined to bring about a reassessment of the pessimistic conclusions that have been summarised above. First, detailed criticisms of the American studies from both American (e.g. Dyer 1968) and British commentators have considerably affected the confidence which could be placed in the great majority of the earlier studies. These used, it was argued, only a very limited number of measures of the school environment in their analyses, thereby increasing the chances that the school would have less effect than the other influences upon pupil life for which many more measures were included. The Coleman analysis used only one measure of school environment (volumes per student in the school library) for their analysis of reading ability at grades 1, 3 and 6; and at grades 9 and 12, the library measure was supplemented merely by one other measure representing the presence or absence of science laboratory facilities. Other commentators (Rutter and Madge 1976) have suggested that the absence of school effects may merely reflect the fact that the variables chosen to measure school quality have usually been of a 'resource-based' variety and have not included detailed assessment of many aspects of within school life (e.g. teacher/pupil relations, school 'ethos' and school organisational structure) that may have important effects upon the nature of pupil outputs. The tests used to measure these pupil outputs were, it was further argued, mostly of verbal or numerical ability and did not usually measure the 'social' outputs of the educational system (e.g. values, attendance rates, delinquency rates, self-perceptions, etc.) on which schools may have had greater effects. Lastly, the technique of analysis used in most of the early studies was multiple regression, in which a series of sets of variables are entered into the analysis in logical sequence, thereby permitting an estimate of the total variance that is due to the effect of the different sets of variables. The usual ordering for the entry of the variables into the regression equation was *family variables*, *community variables* and *school variables*, in sequence, with such an analysis usually showing, as mentioned above, that 20 or 30 per cent of the variance was explicable by the first two sets of variables, and perhaps only 3 to 5 per cent by the set of school variables. If there was a high intercorrelation between the set of family and the set of school variables, however, much of the variation that might have been due to school variables would have been exhausted after the prior entry of the family variables. This, it has been argued, led to an artificially low estimate of school effects.

The second set of factors that has prompted a reassessment of the studies arguing for limited school effects have been generated by further analyses of the data bases of the studies themselves. Such analyses suggest that, first, the schools in the Coleman Report had a quite marked effect on children as they grew into adolescence; and secondly, the effects of school factors at all age groups was substantial for the groups of low ability, low social class and non-white children, though not for others. Thirdly, school factors were also shown in the Coleman data to be very highly intercorrelated with certain of the 'non-cognitive' outcomes of the educational process – Mayeste's re-analysis shows a multiple correlation of 0.59 between sense of control (re-labelled by him 'attitude towards life') and an optimum combination of 31 school variables, which do not include characteristics of the student body (see Dyer 1968 for further details).

The belief in the ineffectiveness of schooling as a medium of social change has also been challenged by the appearance of an increasing number of studies from the United States and Britain that indicate, contrary to earlier suggestions, the existence of substantial school effects upon pupil outcomes of all kinds. Discussion of these findings, indicating their overall coherence and their implications for school policy and future research are the subject of the remainder of this chapter.

The American Studies

One of the first American studies to demonstrate substantial school effects was that of Goodman (1959), who showed that a higher per pupil expenditure, a good ratio of special staff and the existence of a more 'child-centred' classroom atmosphere were all positively associated with students' 'composite achievement' at grade 7. The well-known *Project Talent* studies by Shaycroft (1967) of a cohort of over 6,000 pupils passing through high school also suggested that on all but two of the forty-two measures of student attainment used, student gains in knowledge varied significantly from school to school. Although Shaycroft claimed that students in some schools learnt more, or improved their ability more than in other schools, the sources of these differences apparently resisted easy identification.

Subsequent work by McDill and his associates (1967, 1973) built on these earlier studies by suggesting that the key factors that accounted for the differential effectiveness of American high schools were to be found in the social climates of these institutions themselves. Crucially, these factors appeared to affect student academic performance even when the differences in socio-economic composition between schools had been parcelled out; as McDill concludes:

> the findings lead to the tentative conclusion that in those schools where academic competition, intellectualism and subject matter competence are emphasised and rewarded by faculty and student bodies, individual students tend to conform to the scholastic norms of the majority and achieve at a higher level. (p. 199)

Although McDill and his associates were unable in these studies to determine those factors that had generated the different value climates of over-achieving and under-achieving schools, subsequent work by Weber, by the New York State Office of Education, by Madden and by Brookover and Lezotte has begun to unravel the complexity of within-school life and suggest the factors in this area that may have effects upon pupil development that the above studies have noted. Weber (1971) focused upon the characteristics of four inner-city schools in which the children's reading ability was clearly above national norms. All four schools had 'strong leadership' from their principals – all also had high expectations for their students. All the schools had 'an orderly, relatively quiet and pleasant atmosphere' and all had 'a strong emphasis upon pupil acquisition of reading skills and on evaluation of pupil progress'.

The subsequent New York State Office of Education Performance Review (1974) confirmed many of Weber's findings in its study of a high-performance and a low-performance school, each one taking from a similar, predominantly poor population. This study suggested that:

– the differences in student performance in these two schools seemed to be attributable to factors under the schools' control;
– administrative behaviour, policies and practices in the schools appeared to have a significant impact on school effectiveness;
– the more effective inner-city school was led by an administrative team which provided a good balance between management and instructional skills;
– the administrative team in the more effective school had developed a plan for dealing with the reading problem and had implemented the plan throughout the school.
– classroom reading instruction did not appear to differ between the

two schools since classroom teachers in both schools had problems
in teaching reading and assessing pupils' reading skills;
— many professional personnel in the less effective school
attributed children's reading problems to non-school factors and
were pessimistic about their ability to have an impact, creating an
environment in which children failed because they were not
expected to succeed. However, in the more effective school,
teachers were less sceptical about their ability to have an impact
on children: children responded to unstimulating learning
experiences predictably – they were apathetic, disruptive or
absent.

The importance of the *leadership role*, of *staff expectations* and of the
general *'school ethos'* in affecting pupil performance that is evident in
the work of McDill, Weber and in the above study is also confirmed by
the Californian work of Madden and associates (1976). Their study of
21 'high-achieving' schools and 21 'low-achieving' schools (matched on
the basis of having similar pupil characteristics at entry) revealed a
number of important differences, for example:

(1) In comparison to teachers at lower-achieving schools, teachers
at higher-achieving schools reported that their principals
provided them with a significantly greater amount of support.

(2) Teachers in higher-achieving schools were more task-oriented
in their classroom approach and exhibited more evidence of
applying appropriate principles of learning than did teachers
in lower-achieving schools.

(3) In comparison to teachers at lower-achieving schools, teachers
at higher-achieving schools reported higher levels of access to
'outside the classroom' materials.

(4) Teachers at higher-achieving schools rated district administration
higher on support services.

(5) In comparison to grouping practices at lower-achieving schools, the
higher-achieving schools divided classrooms into fewer groups
for purposes of instruction.

(6) Teachers in higher-achieving schools reported being more
satisfied with various aspects of their work than did teachers in
lower-achieving schools.

The Michigan work of Brookover and Lezotte (1976) is the last American
study we consider here and its importance lies in the support it gives to

the main findings of the earlier studies we have noted. Analysis of the test results of all Michigan school children in grades 4 and 7 was used to identify elementary schools characterised by 'improving' or by 'declining' pupil performance, schools which were subsequently visited by trained interviewers to assess the nature of their educational and social life.

Analysis suggested, amongst other things, that:

(1)   The improving schools are clearly different from the declining schools in the emphasis their staff places on the accomplishment of the basic reading and mathematics objectives. The improving schools accept and emphasise the importance of these goals and objectives while declining schools give much less emphasis to such goals and do not specify them as fundamental.

(2)   There is a clear contrast in the evaluations that teachers and principals make of the students in the improving and declining schools. The staffs of the improving schools tend to believe that *all* of their students can master the basic objectives; and furthermore, the teachers perceive that the principal shares this belief. They tend to report higher and increasing levels of student ability, while the declining school teachers project the belief that students' ability levels are low and, therefore, they cannot master even these objectives.

(3)   The staff of the improving schools hold decidedly higher and apparently increasing levels of expectations with regard to the educational accomplishments of their students. In contrast, staff of the declining schools are much less likely to believe that their students will complete high school or college.

(4)   The teachers and principals of the improving schools are much more likely to assume responsibility for teaching the basic reading and mathematics skills and are much more committed to doing so. The staffs of the declining schools feel there is not much that teachers can do to influence the achievement of their students. They tend to displace the responsibility for skill-learning on to the parents or the students themselves.

(5)   There seems to be a clear difference in the principal's role in the improving and declining schools. In the improving schools, the principal is more likely to be an instructional leader, to be more assertive in his instructional leadership role, is more of a disciplinarian and perhaps most of all, assumes responsibility for

the evaluation of the achievement of basic objectives. The
principals in the declining schools appear to be permissive and
to emphasise informal and collegial relationships with the
teachers. They put more emphasis on general public relations
and less emphasis upon evaluation of the school's effectiveness
in providing a basic education for the students.

(6) The improving-school staffs appear to evidence a greater
degree of acceptance of the concept of accountability. Certainly
they accept the results of Michigan State tests as one indication
of their effectiveness to a much greater degree than the
declining-school staffs. The latter tend to reject the relevance
of the testing programme and make little use of these assessment
devices as a reflection of their instruction. (Michigan was running
a comprehensive Educational Assessment Program.)

The conclusions of these American studies are to some extent reflected
in the growing number of British research projects which have also
stressed the importance of the individual school's own influence upon
pupil development.

The British Studies

One of the most influential of the British studies on the effects of
schooling was the important work of Power (1967, 1972) undertaken
in the secondary schools of Tower Hamlets. In an article entitled somewhat provocatively *Delinquent Schools?*, published in 1967, Power
argued that the large differences between his sample of schools in their
delinquency rates for boys – from 0.7 per cent to 17 per cent of pupils
officially delinquent per annum – may well have reflected variation in
the effects of the local secondary modern schools themselves, given the
relatively homogeneous nature of the communities that they served. In
part because of the furore triggered off by the publication of this
article, Power and his team were never able to pursue their investigations
into the schools themselves. Subsequent criticisms of the methodology
by which Power claimed to show the independence of the schools'
delinquency rates from the delinquency rates of their catchment areas
(Baldwin 1972), and later evidence from the longitudinal Cambridge
Institute of Criminology study suggesting that high-delinquency-rate
schools in their London sample were merely reflecting the high levels of
delinquency proneness in their intakes (Farrington 1973), combined to

cast strong doubts upon the validity of Power's hypotheses of substantial school effects.

Although the publication of findings by Gath (1972, 1977) suggesting substantial variation in the child-guidance referral rates and delinquency rates of schools taking from similar catchment areas, and the publication of preliminary findings by Rutter (1973) showing a substantial variation in the behavioural-deviance rates of pupils at London primary schools hinted at the existence of school effects of a moderate size, it is probably the work in South Wales by ourselves and our associates, and the continued work in London by Rutter and his associates that has been most influential in leading to a re-assessment of the former evidence from Britain and America that schools made little difference to the level of development of their pupils.

The work of Rutter (1979) was undertaken in a sample of twelve London comprehensive schools and was concerned to answer two linked questions: first, whether or not the different schools had a differential effect upon their pupils and secondly, if they did, what factors within the schools could account for these differences? Four different indicators of school output were selected – *delinquency, attendance, within-school behaviour* and *public examination results* – and the considerable variation that was found between the schools in their performance on these measures remained even after differences between the schools in the quality of their pupil intake were taken into account. Furthermore, schools tended to perform consistently 'well' or consistently 'badly' on all four of the measures of school output.

Detailed investigation of the internal organisation, within-school processes, school ethos and teacher/pupil interaction within the twelve institutions suggested that physical aspects of the schools, such as size or the age of the buildings were not important determinants of output, and that further variation in the nature of the formal academic organisation, formal pastoral-care organisation, pupil/teacher ratio and size of classes also appeared to make little difference to school outcomes.

In a recent discussion of these findings (Rutter 1980), the important within-school influences upon school outcome were stated to be:

(i)   The balance of intellectually able and less-able children in the school since, when a preponderance of pupils in a school were likely to be unable to meet the expectations of scholastic success, peer group cultures with an anti-academic or anti-authority emphasis may have formed.

(ii) The system of rewards and punishments – ample use of
rewards, praise and appreciation being associated with
favourable outcomes.

(iii) School environment: good working conditions, responsiveness
to pupil needs and good care and decoration of buildings were
associated with better outcomes.

(iv) Ample opportunities for children to take responsibility and to
participate in the running of their school lives appeared conducive to favourable outcome.

(v) Successful schools tended to make good use of homework, to
set clear academic goals and to have an atmosphere of
confidence as to their pupils' capacities.

(vi) Outcomes were better where teachers provided good models of
behaviour by means of good time-keeping and willingness to
deal with pupil problems.

(vii) Findings upon group management in the classroom suggested
the importance of preparing lessons in advance, of keeping the
attention of the whole class, of unobtrusive discipline, of a
focus on rewarding good behaviour and of swift action to
deal with disruption.

(viii) Outcomes were more favourable when there was a combination
of firm leadership together with a decision-making process in
which all teachers felt that their views were represented.

The above research has, of course, been subjected to vigorous criticism
from many sources (e.g. Hargreaves 1980; Goldstein 1980; Acton 1980).
It has been alleged that the study over-estimated the effect of the
schools upon their output-measures because only two measurements
(pupil ability and pupil occupational group) of the quality of the school
intakes were used, thereby under-estimating the variance that might
have been explicable by other intake factors. It is also alleged that insufficient attention was given to possible important factors such as
curriculum content and the relationships between teachers and pupils
that may also have been responsible for differential school effects.
Nevertheless, it seems likely that the authors' conclusion (Rutter *et al.*
1979, p. 205) that 'the results carry the strong implication that schools
can do much to foster good behaviour and attainment and that even in
a disadvantaged area schools can be a force for the good' is still substantially correct.

Our own work in South Wales, although undertaken in a group of
secondary modern schools and in a relatively homogenous former
mining valley that is very different in its community patterns from the
communities of Inner London, has produced findings that in certain
ways are parallel to those of Rutter and his team. Our work involved
the collection of data on the pupil inputs, pupil outputs and school
processes of eight secondary schools, each of which was taking the
bottom two-thirds of the ability range from a clearly delineated catchment area. We found substantial differences in the quality of the school
outputs from the eight schools when we began our work in 1974, with
a variation in the delinquency rate of from 3.8 per cent per annum to
10.5 per cent; in the attendance rate of from 77.2 per cent average
attendance to 89.1 per cent; and in the academic attainment rate of
from 8.4 per cent proceeding to the local technical college to 52.7 per
cent proceeding on to further education.

Our early analysis (Reynolds 1976; Reynolds *et al.* 1976) of our
intake data showed no tendency for the schools with the higher levels
of performance to be receiving more-able intakes on entry – in fact,
high overall school performance was associated with lower-ability intakes
as measured by the Ravens Standard Progressive Matrices test of non-
verbal ability. Although subsequent full analysis of our full range of
intake data reveals a tendency for the higher-performance schools to
have intakes of pupils with higher verbal and numerical ability, the
personality variables for these intakes (higher extraversion and higher
neuroticism scores) suggest on the contrary a poor educational prognosis.
Simply, the intake scores still seem to be unable to explain the variation
between our schools.

Detailed observation of the schools from 1974 to 1977 and the
collection of a wide range of material concerned with pupils' attitudes
to school, teachers' perceptions of pupils, within-school organisation,
resource levels, etc. (for further information see Reynolds *et al.* 1981)
has revealed a number of factors within the school that are associated
with more 'effective' regimes. These include a high proportion of pupils
in authority positions (as in the Rutter study), low levels of institutional
control, low rates of physical punishment, small overall size, more
favourable teacher/pupil ratios and more tolerant attitudes to the
enforcing of certain rules regarding 'dress, manners and morals' (see
Reynolds (1975) for further information on this point).

Crucially, our observation has revealed differences between the
schools in the ways that they have attempted to mobilise pupils towards
the acceptance of their predetermined goals. Such differences seem to

fall within the parameters of one or other of two major strategies, *'coercion'* or *'incorporation'*. Five of the eight schools that took part in the research appeared to be utilising the incorporative strategy to a greater (three schools) or lesser (two schools) extent. The major components of this strategy are two-fold: the incorporation of pupils into the organisation of the school and the incorporation of their parents into support of the school.

Pupils were incorporated within the classroom by encouraging them to take an active and participative role in lessons and by letting them intervene verbally without the teacher's explicit directions. Pupils in schools which used this strategy were also far more likely to be allowed and encouraged to work in groups than their counterparts in schools utilising the coercive strategy. Outside formal lesson time, attempts were made to incorporate pupils into the life of the school in other ways. One of these was the use of numbers of pupil prefects and monitors, from all parts of the ability range, whose role was largely one of supervision of other pupils in the absence of staff members. Such a practice appeared to have the effect of inhibiting the growth of anti-school pupil cultures because of its effect in creating senior pupils who were generally supportive of the school. It also had the latent and symbolic function of providing pupils with a sense of having some control over their within-school lives; the removal of these symbols also gave the school a further sanction it could utilise against its deviants.

Another means of incorporation into the values and norms of the school was the development of *inter*personal rather than *im*personal relationships between teachers and pupils. Basically, teachers in these incorporative schools attempted to tie pupils into the value-systems of the school and of the adult society by means of developing 'good' personal relationships with them. In effect, the judgement was made in these schools that internalisation of teacher-values was more likely to occur if pupils saw teachers as 'significant others' deserving of respect. Good relationships were consequent upon minimal use of overt institutional control (so that pupil behaviour was relatively unconstrained), low rates of physical punishment, a tolerance of a limited amount of 'acting out' (e.g. smoking, gum chewing), a pragmatic hesitancy to enforce rules which might have provoked rebellion, and an attempt to reward good behaviour rather than punish bad behaviour. Within this school ethos, instances of pupil 'deviance' evoked therapeutic – rather than coercive – responses from within the school. Attempts to incorporate pupils were paralleled by attempts to enlist the support of their parents by the establishment of close, informal or semi-formal relations between teachers and parents, the encouraging of informal visits to the school and the frequent and full provision of information to parents that concerns pupil progress and governor and staff decisions.

In contrast, schools which utilised the coercive strategy to a greater or lesser extent (three of the eight schools), made no attempt to incorporate pupils into the authority structure of the school, an action which would have been seen by them as akin to Montgomery inviting Rommel to become one of his staff officers. Furthermore, these schools made no attempt to invite the support of parents, because the teachers believed that no support would be forthcoming. They exhibited high levels of institutional control, strict rule enforcement, high rates of physical punishment and very little tolerance of any 'acting out'. The idea — as in the incorporative schools — of establishing some kind of 'truce' with pupils in these schools was anathema, since the teachers perceived that the pupils would necessarily abuse such an arrangement. Pupil deviance was expeditiously punished and within the overall social context of these schools, this was entirely understandable: therapeutic concern would have had little effect because pupils would have had little or no respect for the teacher-therapist.

The most likely explanation of the choice of different strategies is to be found in the differences (in the two groups of schools) in the teacher perceptions of their intakes. In schools which have adopted a coercive strategy, there is a consistent tendency to over-estimate the proportion of pupils whose background can be said to be 'socially deprived'; in one such school teachers thought these children accounted for 70 per cent of their intake, whilst in one of the incorporative schools teachers put the proportion only at 10 per cent. Similarly there is a consistent tendency to under-estimate their pupils' ability. In these coercive schools, teachers regard pupils as being in need of 'character training' and 'control' which stems from a deficiency in primary socialisation, a deficiency which the school attempts to make good by a form of custodialism. Such perceptions are germane to the creation of a school ethos of coercion.

This variance between the teaching staffs of the two different groups of schools is wide and bears, as we have seen, virtually no correspondence with the reality (insofar as we are able to define 'reality') of their situation. If the crucial factor in the generation of different school strategies is — as we believe — perceptions amongst teachers, then a plausible explanation would seem to be offered by the notion that the process at work in the 'coercive schools' is one where, to use William

Ryan's apt phrase, teachers 'blame their victims'. What appears to be happening is that the staffs at the coercive schools externalise their failure by identifying their pupils as of less potential and as 'under-socialised'. Once such perceptions are generated, they are passed on to incoming teachers and incoming pupils, resulting in changes of values and of behaviour for both groups.

Conclusion

We have attempted to re-assert in this chapter a belief in the importance of schooling and schools as determinants of adolescent ability, adolescent behaviour and adolescent social development. Whereas conclusions were drawn from the experience of failure of many of the educational reforms that reflected unfavourably upon the possibility of securing effective changes by means of social engineering through the educational system, our re-assessment of the evidence suggests that many educational changes were of organisational form rather than inter-personal or educational substance, and that many more 'micro'-level changes in curriculum and teaching methods were, mostly because of inadequate preparation and hasty implementation, changes only of a minor nature.

As well as seeing the failure of educational reforms as reflecting defects in the policies themselves and believing that policies of a different kind – maybe on the lines of some suggested elsewhere in this book – may still attain much valued educational and social goals, we have argued that the body of literature that is held to show that schools make little difference to the nature of their pupils, is itself seriously flawed in its methodological adequacy. And we have quoted from the extensive body of knowledge that is now emerging in Britain and the United States which suggests the existence both of substantial school-effects and a range of factors common to both cultures that appear responsible for such effects. At the same time, further re-analysis of the IEA studies (Coleman 1975) showing substantial school-system effects on attainment, (except in England where the variance explained was minimal!), and further evidence suggesting that programmes of compensatory education were effective in certain cases (Halsey 1980) and that resource-levels had a strong impact upon educational attainments (Byrne and Williamson 1975), have combined with the factors mentioned earlier to affirm again the importance of the educational environment of the school.

For further successful development of this new paradigm within educational research, however, it is necessary to expand our knowledge in new directions and areas. First, we need more research on the effects of secondary schools – such as 'progressive' secondary schools – other than the London comprehensives and South Wales comprehensives and secondary modern schools that research in this country has been confined to so far; the effects on children of various types of primary schools could also be explored further. Such research would enable us to discover if the important 'school factors' so far delineated also apply in other educational settings. Secondly, we need to discover if schools have differential effects upon *different groups* of children, such as the able, the less able and ethnic minorities; and we need to discover whether the same school factors act in the same way on such different groupings. Thirdly, we need to discover the relative strength of school and home factors in determining educational outcomes.

Most important of all, we need to further investigate the precise mechanisms by which the schools mediate their effects and, crucially, the key factors which generate such differences between schools. Are the differences between schools in their educational potency reflecting a variation in the ideologies of the personnel in the institutions, or do they reflect merely pragmatic situational adaptations? Are the differences actually *reflecting* past differences between schools in their effectiveness? Once such questions are explored, we shall have much useful information of direct relevance to those wishing to modify the 'micro'-level of the school classroom and the more 'macro'-level of the school in its relationship to the local community.

All we can say with confidence at the present time is that change in the nature of the products of secondary schooling is unlikely to be attained simply by modifying the formal organisation, the resource-levels, the teaching methods and the curriculum content that much past reform has focused on, since it seems that these factors are not the important determinants of outputs from schools in Britain and America. It is much more likely that the key to successful modification of school practice is to be found in the 'phenomenological' world of schooling – in the *perceptions* that teachers in different schools have of their pupils, in the *interpersonal relations* and mutual perceptions of teachers, and in the mutual interpersonal perceptions that govern pupil and teacher relations. Particular forms of organisation and practice may facilitate 'good' attitudes and relationships, but both the American and British studies that have been reported suggest that it is the 'culture' of schools rather than their structure that needs to be the focus for our efforts at reform. Whilst structural change at a classroom or school level is likely to affect attitudes and perceptions, successful modification of school environments may well necessitate direct forms of intervention in the social relations of school life.

4 DIFFERENCES BETWEEN SCHOOLS: THE IMPLICATIONS FOR SCHOOL PRACTICE

Janet Ouston

The detailed reviews of recent studies on school-effects (Chapter 3) have shown that, on a limited range of indicators of development, differences between schools cannot be entirely explained by differences in the characteristics of the pupils. Even after statistical allowances have been made for differences in measured ability and family background at the end of primary schooling, secondary schools still vary considerably in their examination pass-rates, in delinquency-rates, in rates of attendance and in patterns of behaviour at school. In general, schools which are successful on one outcome also tend to be successful on the other three.

In our own study of twelve London secondary schools (Rutter, Maughan, Mortimore, Ouston and Smith 1979) we were able to look at possible relationships between the school's performance on our indicators of outcome and the characteristics of the schools as social institutions. The first finding that there were no direct relationships between physical features of the schools, such as their size or the age of the buildings, and outcome, nor between resources and outcome, may be regarded by many as surprising. As the London schools were all run by the same local authority (hence had similar financial support) the large differences between them could not be explained by differences in resources. Again, the successful schools were not the ones with the smallest classes or the most favourable teacher/pupil ratio. Within the range which existed across the twelve schools, features of this kind could not account for all the differences between them.

Our second set of findings relates to the balance of the intake to the schools. The twelve schools involved in the study were all serving a predominantly disadvantaged inner-city population with fewer intellectually able children than London as a whole. About half of these able children transferred to selective or independent schools so that the secondary schools in our study were all admitting a considerably less able population than other, more favoured areas of the city. It seemed that having a very adverse balance was an additional handicap for a school, the presence of more able children correlating with more successful outcomes for all groups of children. As none of the schools

had a socially advantaged and intellectually able intake we were not
able to look at both ends of the spectrum of balance, hence the interpretations of our findings are again limited by the relatively narrow range
of differences between the schools.

Our third set of findings are concerned with the differences between
the more and less successful schools in their day-to-day functioning, and
in the typical styles of interaction between children and teachers which
had developed at each school. We found that the more successful schools
were likely to emphasise the academic side of school life, to praise and
encourage pupils' good work and to maintain the pupils' direct involvement
in lessons. These schools also provided a better physical environment
for their pupils and encouraged them both to participate in school
activities and to take responsibility at school. The successful schools
combined higher expectations of academic success with appreciation
of pupils' achievements, whilst providing a pleasant and supportive
environment. Full details of the findings are given in Rutter *et al.* (1979)
and are also discussed in Maughan *et al.* (1980 in press).

Taken together, the results of this study along with others reviewed
by Reynolds and Sullivan, suggest that a school's performance is not
totally predetermined by features which lie outside its own control.
Although both the characteristics of the children admitted to the
schools and the balance of the intake relate to outcome, school practice
also appears to have a measurable effect on children's development.

Implications of the Research for Teachers

Findings of differences in outcome between schools and on the relationship between these and school practice, have two immediate implications
for teachers. First of all, they support the belief that what goes on at
school has a real impact on the lives of the pupils. Our findings on
examination pass-rates and on delinquency show how very similar
ten-year-olds can have quite different achievements at the age of
sixteen, depending upon the particular school attended. This is not to
deny the powerful influence of home background and academic ability
on achievement in adolescence, but they are clearly not the whole story:
school, also, can be more or less influential. Secondly, the emerging
pattern of relationships between school practice and outcome (see Chapter
3) highlights some of the areas which may be particularly important in
the running of a well-functioning secondary school, thus indicating where
innovation might be worthwhile.

If school does 'make a difference' to children's development, how can teachers ensure that their school is actually doing as well as it can for the pupils in its care? In simple terms, we can ask: what should schools be doing to make themselves more effective, how can they bring this about, and how will they know whether or not they have been successful?

There has been considerable interest over the last few years in the curriculum, to the extent that some educationalists have seen this as the only way of improving education for the majority of children. Whilst our own work in no way denies the importance of the curriculum, it is more concerned with other aspects of the school – what might broadly be considered under the heading of 'school as a social institution' – where a large number of adults and children have to work together for a large part of their year. Schools which manage to achieve at least a moderate level of successful functioning seem more likely to develop the curriculum and to try out new approaches to learning. In contrast, schools which are overwhelmed by daily problems may not have sufficiently high morale or energy to be able to risk exploring new ideas and new curricula. Our research suggests that concern with both sides of school life, with the curriculum *and* with the school climate more generally, will have the most beneficial results for the school.

However, research findings should not be implemented without first translating them to meet the needs of the particular school concerned; for example, the successful schools in our study displayed pupils' work on the classroom walls and set regular homework. This should not be interpreted as a direct prescription for action, but as evidence of a concern with academic work. It would be naïve to expect huge improvements in a school's performance to result simply from covering the school walls with children's work and issuing all teachers and pupils with a homework timetable! Such differences are merely indicators of the school's emphasis and it is these underlying factors rather than the items themselves, that are important. Schools in different circumstances might realise their academic aims in quite different ways.

How, then, can studies of school differences be useful to teachers? They can, perhaps, serve several different functions; first of all, by suggesting areas where innovation might be worthwhile and, conversely, lowering the priorities which might be given to other areas. A school concerned with problems in the classroom might, alongside consideration of the curriculum, also look at the opportunities provided for less experienced teachers to develop skills in classroom management. From the children's point of view issues such as the ratio of praise and punishment could also be considered in the context of the classroom. Does the school actually create opportunities to show appreciation of children's achievements rather than being predominantly concerned with punishing poor behaviour? The successful schools in our study created a pleasant environment for teaching and learning. The school buildings were well kept and attractive, regardless of age; graffiti were removed and damage quickly repaired. In contrast, several of the less successful schools provided a very drab environment for their staff and pupils, with walls bare except for graffiti and widespread damage. Again, the importance of such features in school life is not so much in the direct effect they have on pupils as in their indirect effect on the school as a whole.

Although none of these ideas is new, a comparative study allows us to examine them in a different context, seeing which of a whole range of good ideas actually relate to successful outcome and which do not. One of the findings in this latter category relates to the efforts which some schools make to ensure that pupils keep the same teacher in each subject from year to year. We found that continuity of this kind was unrelated to outcome, suggesting that it might not be as important as many teachers had thought. There are several possible explanations of this interesting finding but it seems likely that continuity of curriculum was as important as continuity of the teaching staff. Teachers in the more successful schools reported working with others in their department on planning pupils' work, whereas in the less successful schools teachers were much more isolated from one another; there was little overall co-ordination between teachers in their teaching programme. Had these schools managed to achieve their aim of keeping a teacher with one group throughout the school the need for joint planning might have been reduced, but in fact none of these schools attained this level of continuity so the possible benefits were lost. A second explanation might be that, inevitably, some pupils and teachers do not work well together: different personalities clash and some pupils respond to a teaching style which does not suit others. These pupils are likely to suffer by being taught for several years by a teacher they may not like, whereas annual change of teacher (with a well-planned curriculum) avoids problems of this kind. Here then, an unexpected finding from a comparative study suggests that it might be worth placing less emphasis on continuity from year to year if this makes it possible to timetable regular departmental meetings.

Methods of introducing change will obviously depend to a certain extent on the existing pattern of decision-making within an individual school. Studies of educational innovation have been mainly concerned with the evaluation of new curricula, or the actual implementation of progressive educational ideas. In both types of studies the focus is on the implementation and follow-up of innovation rather than on the initial decision to introduce a new curriculum or continue using existing programmes. A common finding from studies of innovation is that far less change actually occurs than educationalists expect; teachers, like most other professionals, are slow to alter their established practices. Whiteside (1978) suggests that there is a widely held myth relating to the extent of educational innovation which is rarely supported by studies of current practice (see also Galton *et al.* 1980).

The patterns of innovation which are under consideration here are, however, rather different from those focused on the curriculum or style of presentation, in that they are concerned with a large section of a school rather than one department only. Successful school-wide innovation is quite difficult to achieve, partly because of the natural resistance to change which is found in all organisations (see Glen 1975) but also because of the traditional autonomy of the teacher. Changes in school practice may be more effective if they are started in one area of the school – perhaps one year group of pupils – where the new ideas are actively supported. If they are successful on a limited scale then other teachers and children may want to take part. By approaching the innovation piecemeal, it can be tailored to the needs of the school by those who are enthusiastic, then taken up by others after it has proved valuable. Since children are often almost as resistant to change as adults, it might be more sensible to introduce change in the first year, continuing with each new group of pupils so that, in effect, a change of practice would take five years to become school wide. This style of systems change will not avoid damaging conflict entirely but may help to reduce anxiety by allowing ample time for staff to discuss the proposed changes and to participate in the decision process. This pattern is often used in the introduction of mixed-ability teaching, but could be successfully adopted for other innovations.

Research on the introduction of change in organisations outside education has highlighted several areas of difficulty which may be particularly relevant to schools. Even after the decision to introduce a new scheme has been taken, there may be confusion about the details of its implementation, which in turn can lead to both pupils and staff feeling dissatisfied. A new idea for awarding merit marks to first year pupils, for example, may founder because teachers are interpreting it

in many different ways. A related problem is that of keeping
enthusiasm for a new scheme going long enough for it to become an
established part of school practice. Regular discussions will certainly
help, as will more informal feedback from other teachers and pupils.
In many schools the role of co-ordinator of a new programme will be
taken by a senior member of staff, perhaps a head of year or department,
but the school's educational psychologist could also become a valuable
extra resource. His knowledge and experience of practice in different
schools and his training in research can be useful both at the implementation and evaluation stages.

Individual schools have, traditionally, rarely been concerned with
assessing the consequences of change. It has often been argued that the
objectives of schooling are too diverse and too intangible to be evaluated.
There are, however, many different approaches to evaluation, none of
which provide a definitive answer but which used together may
provide background information for subsequent decisions. Many
examples of this approach are given by Shipman (1979). If we take the
issue of the continuity of teachers from year to year, it would be quite
possible to monitor some of the results of a change in this area in several
different ways. It would almost certainly be valuable to consider the
possibility that the children had learned less after a change of subject
teacher, using either a standardised test or one specially devised by the
school. Children who had been taught by the same teacher over several
years could then be compared with those who had experienced two or
three teachers in the same time period. But it would be at least as
important to consider other implications of a change of this kind: do
the pupils prefer remaining with the same teacher, and do the teachers
find it less rewarding to change classes annually? What effects does less
continuity of teachers have on the pastoral side of school life, on the
level of disruptive behaviour, and on curriculum development?
Assuming that the school had, at the same time as reducing continuity,
introduced regular departmental meetings, it would be important to
consider their value. Had they been used constructively or did most
teachers find them a waste of time? Had it been possible to work on
the curriculum as well as solve more immediate problems? Did
probationary teachers find them a useful part of their in-service training?

Drawing all these points together into an informal evaluation of the
impact of such a change would raise many important issues for the
school. One of these would almost certainly be the observation that
some teachers, or even some departments, were much more successful
than others in working with the new system. This finding, in its turn,

could have two outcomes, either that the needs of particular departments were different, or that those who were less successful could be helped by others who had developed more effective ways of coping with the demands of the new pattern of teaching. Many other innovations in school could be considered using a comparable approach, without in any way over-simplifying or devaluing the complex process of schooling.

Implications for Educational Psychologists and other Professional Groups

In recent years educational psychologists have become more concerned with working with schools, moving away from their traditional concern with the problems of individual children and their families (Burden 1978). The results of comparative studies of schools which stress the schools' contribution to the development of individual children, add support to this change in emphasis. Our own finding that patterns of behaviour at secondary school are almost independent of behaviour at primary school suggests that schools do have a powerful influence on children during adolescence, although longer-term effects have still to be demonstrated.

This change in focus from the individual to the school, should not, however, be so widespread as to ignore the needs of individual pupils. Children's problems at school may be a consequence of family or personal difficulties and be quite unrelated to the school, but it would almost certainly be true that a large number of 'difficult' children are responding to weaknesses in their school rather than to severe family problems. Successful schools appear to *prevent* too many difficulties from arising rather than being exceptionally skilled in dealing with them once they have occurred. In these schools new pupils enter an environment which is calm and supportive, where the older pupils are both successful and well behaved and where teachers have no need to be excessively concerned with discipline. Given such circumstances even children with very stressful lives outside school can make good progress. New teachers, also, have many advantages in such a school. They are not constantly trying to maintain order but have time and energy to develop both their own teaching skills and their programmes of work. In contrast, less successful schools set poor models of behaviour; teachers have to put more emphasis on control, possibly creating a much more provocative climate; children see little possibility of success and the depressing cycle of disruptive behaviour and academic failure is perpetuated.

There are obvious difficulties for the educational psychologist who seeks to be an agent of change. Schools with problems of the type discussed here often have poor links with external agencies – it is the more successful school which has the energy and confidence to ask for help from outside. Educational psychologists, too, tend to work in schools which ask for their help since they see this as a better use of their own limited resources. Before psychologists can start work in these more isolated schools, teachers need to extend the expectations they have of the psychologist's skills and interests. The psychologists, too, have to learn to work in a way which may be quite different from their traditional pattern, spending .much more time at school focusing on the whole organisation rather than on individual teachers and pupils, and on being concerned with general issues as much as with particular problems. Although changes in school practice will be made by teachers themselves, the educational psychologist as an 'informed outsider' can offer skills which teachers may not have. His knowledge of educational practice will enable him to propose alternative methods of approaching problems, and his training in research may be useful in helping schools to monitor their own performance. At the classroom level, he may be able to help probationary teachers develop their management skills more effectively than a senior teacher can, since the psychologist is independent of the school hierarchy and not involved in assessing the teachers' competence.

At present there is often little contact *between* schools themselves, particularly as far as the classroom teacher is concerned. Teachers' Centres do, of course, help teachers to exchange ideas out of school but there is very little opportunity for them to visit one another during the school day. Educational psychologists, and educational advisers, have an important role to play in the dissemination of good practice. Schools frequently seem to be developing idiosyncratic solutions to common problems with virtually no information about how other schools have solved, or failed to solve, similar difficulties.

What are the implications for other professional groups concerned with education? The London secondary schools study has two general implications for educational administrators. First, the findings on the relationship between the balance of the intake and outcome suggests that this is an important policy issue. The twelve schools taking part in the study had few intellectually able children so that our results cannot be generalised to quite different situations, but the issue is of such importance that it does need examining across a much wider range of schools. If similar findings to our own emerge, it is then clearly important to identify the way in which the balance of the intake affects the outcome of the pupils. In specific terms, why does a very poor reader entering secondary school do better in a school where there are few other similar children? Is it because more time is spent on remedial work or that teachers have higher expectations or that the peer group is different?

Secondly, local authority advisers are frequently concerned with the teaching of a particular group of subjects rather than with the wider curriculum which the school provides. It would, perhaps, be possible for them to develop their role and responsibilities so that the particular subject is seen in the context of the school as a whole rather than as an isolated body of knowledge.

Teachers, like inspectors and advisers, are generally subject-orientated, but many teachers in senior positions are not primarily concerned with this aspect of school life. Much of their work involves the management of a large organisation, ensuring that it functions sufficiently well for effective teaching and learning to take place. There are also many school-wide issues, such as the opportunities pupils have to participate in actual school life and to take responsibility for their own learning, which appear to relate to success but are not directly subject based. In-service training for senior teachers would allow them to develop these wider skills which are needed for the running of a happy and successful school. Similarly, the focus of the training of student teachers is usually the specialist subject rather than classroom management skills. It is often assumed that periods of teaching practice cover all that is required in this area, but inexperienced teachers often find this aspect of teaching extremely difficult. An increased emphasis on classroom skills at college, and in-service training at school during the early years of teaching (perhaps along the lines suggested by Marland (1975)) would help teachers to develop strategies of group management, hence allowing them more freedom to teach their subject as they choose.

Implications for Future Research

As the study of school differences is only just beginning, the implications for research are wide ranging. Clearly the findings already published need replicating but, at the same time, extending. As a simple example, Reynolds and Murgatroyd (1977) found that school size was a significant feature in relation to outcome, whereas in our own study it was not. One of the reasons for this apparent contradiction might be that

Reynolds's large schools were actually smaller than the *small* London schools. It is possible that size is important up to about 500 pupils but unimportant beyond that. A detailed examination of the relationship between size and outcome across a wide range of schools would help to resolve this issue. There are other similar questions where a more detailed replication would be very valuable. Studies of this kind would enable us to distinguish between features of school practice which are generally important and those which are only relevant to schools serving a disadvantaged inner-city population.

The second issue which has so far not been examined in detail is that of within-school differences. The focus of comparative studies of schools has, naturally, been on differences between them, but the relationship between school practice and outcome may also be understood by looking at differences within schools over time. We found that, for example, schools where pupils were praised were more successful than other schools with less positive feedback. The only way of testing the causal nature of this relationship is to try to relate changes in amounts of praise to changes in children's behaviour. Most of the correlations between practice and outcome that we identified need examining in a longitudinal context if causal inferences are to be drawn. It is hoped that action research of the kind proposed here, where schools introduce new procedures to improve their own performance, will lead to a better understanding of how effective change can be introduced. The involvement of specialist external agencies will give schools access to extra skills, while at the same time providing information for the agencies themselves on the effectiveness of particular types of innovation and on the use of their own skills.

Thirdly, the model of 'school process' we have used needs elaborating. It explains why schools remain the same but not how, or why, they change. The notion of 'outcome' also needs developing, possibly separating it into three different parts. First of all there are concurrent outcomes which are also part of the school process, so that behaviour at school or attendance are both responses to school but also part of the process of schooling. The second set of outcomes, such as exam results, are rather different from the concurrent outcomes since they can act as a passport to work or further education. The final set — and perhaps the most important — is the relationship between a child's experience at school and his subsequent life as an adult. Young people from our twelve schools are currently being interviewed by Grace Gray one year after leaving school. This survey will show whether different experiences at school have any effect on longer-term outcomes and will also enable us to look at the relationship between schooling, exam qualifications and work.

To summarise: comparative studies of schools have shown that they vary in how successful they are on indicators such as academic attainment, attendance, behaviour at school and delinquency. In general, these differences do not relate to differences in their physical features or their resources, but they do relate to particular aspects of school practice. Successful schools emphasised the academic side of school, provided opportunities for pupils to participate and take responsibility, praised good work and behaviour and provided a pleasant environment. All these findings were considered as indicators of the school's style of interaction with its pupils, as being both causes and consequences of the particular school's 'climate'. Even though the causal links between school practice and outcome are not clear, the findings suggest that innovation in these areas might have positive effects. Changes in school practice will, of course, be undertaken by teachers, but other professionals concerned with education have a valuable role to play both in promoting and in evaluating change.

5 THE RANGE OF SOLUTIONS: A CRITICAL ANALYSIS

Arno Rabinowitz

Problem behaviour itself requires definition but perhaps the simplest and most tautological will suffice: behaviour by children which causes schools and teachers problems in finding solutions. A definition of this sort allows for the range and variety of expectations by schools and is as inclusive as that used by HM Inspectorate in their recent survey of special units for problem children: 'pupils, not formally assessed as in need of special educational treatment, who for a variety of reasons find it difficult to accept the normal framework of life and work in schools' (HMI 1978b).

Excluding special educational treatment requiring formal assessment, the range of solutions currently employed to cope with problem behaviour divides itself into three areas:

- arrangements which take place exclusively within the child's school with teaching provided by the school staff or, occasionally, by visiting teachers;
- arrangements which allow the child to remain in his school for part of the time coupled with part-time attendance at an off-site centre;
- arrangements which require the child to be at a centre, away from his own school, for full-time attendance, without the need for formal assessment or ascertainment and while still remaining on the school roll.

A fourth, less easily delineated solution exists, and is most often considered when there is a partial or complete failure of the range of solutions outlined above. It could, however, equally well pre-empt them. It can only be described as a psychological/system/organisational approach and depends upon a clear view of the organisation within which the problem-behaviour manifests itself. In this approach the tacit assumption of the 'special provision' solutions that problem-behaviour is self-generated and susceptible to individual curative measures, is not accepted. However, it is only by considering the first three approaches in some depth that we can arrive at a meaningful appraisal of this last one. This chapter therefore aims to describe the range of provision (with special reference to the Inner London Educational Authority). The conceptual inadequacies of 'withdrawal units' are dealt with at greater length in Robert Daines' review (Chapter 7).

In-school Systems

The currently fashionable label for these in-school systems is 'sanctuary'. Typically these consist of one or two rooms within a secondary school to which pupils causing problems may be referred. The organisation and function of this provision, existing as it does as a school-based resource, obviously varies as to the same extent that one school varies from another. In the HMI survey of such units in 1977 these were defined, together with off-site units, as simply places in which 'with the benefit of smaller groups and experienced teachers, these children and young people can be helped to continue their education and be prepared for life beyond school'. Local education authorities, replying to a questionnaire from Topping and Quelch (1976), reported widespread agreement on only one common aim of sanctuaries: to return the child to the ordinary school situation. Little mention was made of the need to offer relief to other children and teachers from the difficult behaviour of children referred, or of the conceptual basis for the establishment of, and the regime within, sanctuaries. None mentioned the need for clear identification of the aetiology of children's problems and for specific procedures that should be implemented to respond to and to minimise these problems. The existence of the unit and the goodwill surrounding it seemed to be a sufficient *raison d'être*.

Since sanctuaries are, at most, two classrooms staffed by two teachers with occasionally some ancillary help, it would seem to be self-evident that with this restriction of provision the aims and expectations should be similarly restricted. In fact the units are usually invested with a nominal range of functions bordering on the grandiose. In a survey of sanctuaries in the Inner London Education Authority, one Staff Inspector reported that schools expected their sanctuaries to:

- provide temporary release from the ordinary classroom situation for pupils suffering too much emotional or social stress;
- act as a pressure-releasing situation in which children could ease off or cool down after an episode of disruptive or aggressive behaviour;

- provide an opportunity for observation or screening prior to decisions about the involvement of other supportive agencies;
- provide a situation in which a child be helped to develop self-control or an ability to adapt to the normal classroom;
- provide additional tuition in basic skills for children whose behaviour problems emanate from a failure to learn;
- provide for the simple containment of uncontrollable children;
- provide a re-entry zone for children who have truanted;
- act as a place in which children who have had difficulties in attending a school can be helped to re-attend.

It is not only the inclusiveness of the expectations revealed by this list that is remarkable, but also their general level. It is not unduly cynical to say that since no sanctuary could hope to fulfil them they cannot succeed and, by so doing, allow referring teachers to be proved 'right' by their failures.

The above list of expectations parallels the list of criteria produced by Long and Newman (1961) for intervention by psychologists with individual children. Long and Newman suggest that children require some intervention when they:

- *face reality dangers.* If it looks as though a consequence of a child's behaviour might be injury to himself, some intervention is needed.
- *require psychological protection.* If a child is behaving in a way that means that he might be injured by others in retaliation or might be subject to bullying, then some sort of help will be necessary.
- *need protection against too much excitement.* If situations develop in which children may lose control and feel unhappy about their behaviour later, some intervention is necessary.
- *begin to destroy property.* Protecting property protects people and intervention is therefore necessary – and referral to a sanctuary, as with all the above.
- *look like threatening an ongoing programme.* Once a class is motivated in a particular task and the children have an investment in its outcome, it is not fair to have this ruined by one child.
- *look like producing 'negative contagion'.* Intervention is needed if a child's poor behaviour is likely to influence the behaviour of others.
- *contravene an important school rule.* Intervention is necessary (or

referral to a sanctuary) when behaviour which may not necessarily be dangerous or disturbing nonetheless threatens a rule basic to school policy.

— *are likely to come into conflict with the outside world.* If a child behaves in a delinquent or publicly mischievous way, then some referral to an agency in the school may be necessary in order to show other children that this sort of behaviour cannot be countenanced.

— *are threatening a teacher's inner comfort.* If a child's behaviour makes a teacher angry or anxious, then some intervention is needed (or, in current terms, referral to a sanctuary) to reduce the stress on the teacher.

Long and Newman do not suggest any institutionalised response to the children but rather changes in teacher response, and suggestions are made for individual action by the teacher. This type of individual action now appears less often in the catalogue of appropriate school responses to problem behaviour. The main listing is now the establishment of a unit, haven, refuge or sanctuary to deal with these children. In other words, instead of expecting that the individual teacher should be competent to deal with difficult behaviour, it is now assumed that the school, a complex social institution, should erect mechanisms to cope with its own deviants.

One of the difficulties — the 'polluting devices' (to use Illich's phrase) — that sanctuaries create is the way in which they call into doubt both the need and professional duty of teachers to deal with behaviour which in any way exceeds the internal standards of either teacher or school. Sanctuaries are expected to satisfy a wide range of educational, social and emotional demands. To do this, they have limited resources and limited ranges of initiative and action. But they also serve another purpose. This is seldom exemplified in the case that is made out for their establishment: they act as a receptacle for the problems produced by the institutions in which they exist and provide an emotional balm for the people who are involved in the situation. Instead of there being any need to examine the reasons for a child's misbehaviour, a situation is organised in which these problems can be moved to one side and teachers and others allowed to continue as if the problem had not arisen. In this way the 'fault' is always located in the child and never in the school itself.

This process can be seen in the way two London secondary schools describe the children who may be referred to their units:

School A
- girls who are disruptive in class due to emotional or social reasons only;
- girls who are introverted or isolated;
- girls who have emotional problems associated with a specific learning difficulty;
- girls who require an extension of already existing services or counselling;
- girls who are already diagnosed and who are awaiting a place at an external centre;
- girls whose problems require a more thorough diagnosis.

School B
- girls with serious behaviour problems who need close and constant supervision and who are not merely naughty;
- obviously disturbed girls who are exhibiting abnormal behaviour patterns;
- school phobics and truants;
- abnormally withdrawn girls or girls distressed by particular circumstances;
- girls who have been involved in a violent behaviour outburst.

In fact, both these schools have good well-run units; but in only one school, it will be seen, is there any mention at all of circumstances other than endogenous ones which may be influencing a child's behaviour. Implicitly there is an assumption that a child's unacceptable behaviour is entirely or primarily from within and/or susceptible to curative measures directed at the individual. The explanation of both presumed cause and suitable remedial action is located on just one side of the situational equation. The other person involved in the interpersonal situation — and the context in which they both work — is given a neutral value in the equation and, in effect, absolved of responsibility for behaviour problems when they occur. In this way the sanctuary serves not one, but two purposes. It removes problem children from the class-room and allows the teacher to feel that his competence has not been undermined, and the school to feel that its system is satisfactory for its purposes. By giving the unit a 'caring' title of an ecclesiastical character, apparent natural justice and charity are served at the same time.

If this 'polluting' effect of sanctuaries is to be avoided and the sanctuary enabled to perform a really useful function in a school, it is clear that a number of rules are necessary. From those schools which

have established successful sanctuaries, of benefit to both staff and
children, the ILEA Inspectorate survey suggested five rules of primary
importance:

(1)   The sanctuary should have a clear and limited function, fully
      accepted and understood by the whole staff and consistent
      with the ethos of the entire school.
(2)   This function should be understood by all the teachers and by
      the children of the school.
(3)   Following upon this was the necessity to have the sympathy
      of the whole school staff with the work of the unit and a
      willingness to work with it.
(4)   Close support and co-operation by psychological and welfare
      services was necessary, as well as availability of appropriate
      staff and accommodation.
(5)   A carefully considered and planned procedure for referral,
      educational programme, and return to school, was the final,
      critical factor.

If the function and purpose of the unit is not clearly and comprehensively
understood by staff and children, then the opportunities for deliberate
misunderstanding and misuse will multiply as both staff and children
try to divine the rules that operate. The effect of such a procedure is an
expansion of deliberately explorative misbehaviour by children to see
if this results in a referral, and of over-referral by teachers to discern
which children are acceptable and which children a teacher must
attempt to contain. The consequence is an open, chaotic situation in
which it is impossible for the unit to succeed. Should this happen,
children will feel that they have 'won', with deleterious effects on the
functioning of the school. Teachers will feel that nothing can succeed
with difficult children, and the effects on their morale and willingness
to cope with them will be similarly adverse. The net result, again, is
what Illich (1977) calls 'the self-reinforcing iatrogenic loop analogous to
the escalating destruction generated by the polluting procedures used
as anti-pollution devices' (p. 43).

    This may sound like extravagant language, but many of us engaged in
the development of the helping services have become aware that
'solutions' often create more (or different) problems than they solve.

Part-time Off-site Provision

This is less common than on-site provision and differs in the obvious
respect that it is away from the main school campus so that children
are physically absent from their school for part of the time. It tends to
differ in another important respect as well in that it usually services
more than one school, whereas in-school provision is normally for the
host school only. This difference is important in that off-site provision,
being shared, can avoid some of the internal strife-producing situations
characteristic of school-based units, without separating children entirely
from the curriculum of their normal school. As with on-site units, the
first and most important rule for success is a clear understanding by all
referral agencies of the function of the unit. If schools are enabled to
refer non-selectively then there is a probability that units will receive a
population so heterogeneous as to be unmanageable.

Dr Mary Wilson and Mrs Mary Evans, both formerly of the ILEA
Special Schools Inspectorate, have conducted a survey of off-site units
for the Schools Council. Although their researches cover both part-time
and full-time off-site provision, many of their conclusions apply equally
to both, so that it is worth considering them here.

In a lecture given in June 1978 Dr Wilson outlined the results of her
research: these correspond closely to the criteria for the success of on-
site provision, as well as having relevance for full-time off-site provision.
Units, she reported, should not be set up simply as a means of ridding
schools of troublesome pupils. If they are set up in this way they simply
do not succeed. Teachers in charge of the units and teachers responsible
for referring children must perceive them as designed to improve the
social, emotional and educational adjustment of children, or they will
fail to be effective. Parents (mentioned for the first time in this
context) must agree with the placement and understand its aim.
Continuing contact must be maintained with them and this contact
must have a supportive and explanatory purpose. Without this support,
off-site units have found it almost impossible to be effective. The units
need to be small enough to engender a sense of belonging in the children,
but not so small that there is no social dynamic. There needs, ideally,
to be more than one teacher or adult present and a staff/pupil ratio of
one to seven or eight. Teachers must maintain close contact with their
colleagues in the referring schools and attempt either to replicate or
complement the curriculum of the referring schools.

The similarity of these rules to those required for the success of
on-site units is mentioned both in the HMI report and the investigation

by Topping and Quelch (1976). It would seem clear from the literature and the experience of psychologists working with such units, that these requirements have universal relevance for the kinds of provision considered in the present chapter.

Many local education authorities have long-established provisions for the full or part-time off-site education of problem children; some, notably the Inner London Education Authority, are currently expanding these. The units are variously described as 'school support centres', 'educational guidance units', and so on; such vaguely descriptive names have, of course, the same kind of emotional loading as the 'sanctuaries' in ordinary schools.

Experience has shown that failure has occurred when there have been no well-considered ways of maintaining liaison with referring schools and for returning children to their own schools. Unless there is a pre-condition laid upon referring schools that they should receive children back and not regard placement off site as a final solution, these units tend to 'silt up', so that, effectively, the facility ceases to exist. The cycle is as follows. Problems occur (are created?) within the schools and these problems are referred to off-site units which after a while cannot admit any more. The schools become disaffected because they are used to having a provision for referring children out of the school; pressures build up within them for more provision which is then created – and soon fills up, and so on. In this way many problems of behaviour are apparently coped with, more are created, fewer are solved.

One example, again from within the ILEA, could be cited to demonstrate that such effects are not entirely necessary and that they can be avoided by care in conception and execution. The ILEA has approximately forty-five tutorial classes, sited usually within schools but independent of the host school. These accept children whose behaviour appears to be amenable to change through the provision of part-time help in a small group while continuing to live at home and attend an ordinary school. Children awaiting special educational treatment are not accepted, nor are children who cannot attend their own schools for at least part of the time. Referral to these classes is only through an educational psychologist, using carefully designed forms and guidelines. An educational psychologist supervises the running of each class, and admission and discharge is organised by the teacher responsible, in consultation with the educational psychologist. Children may attend the classes for up to four and a-half days a week: the rest of the time they are expected to be in their own schools. Times and days of attendance are determined through discussion with the teacher in charge and the relevant teacher at the referring school, which may be primary or secondary. The composition of the group at the tutorial class in terms of age and sex is a matter for the teacher in charge who has a day a week free for discussion with schools, clinics and parents. Child Guidance Clinics may refer children, as may any other psychiatric agencies, but in all cases referral must have the formal agreement of the supervising educational psychologist.

The role of the psychologist in this situation is to ensure that the appropriate referral criteria have been adhered to and that there is a clear statement as to exactly why tutorial-class placement is required and what effects attendance is expected to achieve. There is also an expectation that the child will be returned to full-time attendance at his school as soon as this becomes practicable. The result of this considerable organisation has been an extraordinarily stable teaching staff, a good balance of referrals in terms of both quantity and quality, with moderate waiting times and a very high incidence of full-time return to school. An important side-effect, in view of what has been said previously, is that there are few attempts by schools to manipulate either children or the referring agents in order to achieve placement. The criteria for entry are clear, published and strictly observed. A sedulous system of reporting back on the progress of their children ensures that each school remains aware of the whole pattern of development, including the progression back to full-time normal schooling.

Full-time Out-of-school Provision

Of all the provisions currently in use for problem children, this is the easiest to define: premises or units, often serving more than one school, to which children may be referred without formal procedures for full-time education while remaining on the roll of their normal school. The period of attendance may vary according to the nature and purpose of the establishment. The HMI survey commented that such units pose completely different problems compared with units in ordinary schools. For instance, in school sanctuaries admission is at the fiat of the head or senior staff. In off-site units there is an additional controlling factor which makes admission rarely as straightforward as admission to an in-school unit.

Where units serve more than one school, admission is complicated by the varying demands and expectations of contributing schools and by their varying systems for defining and dealing with problem-behaviour, as well as by the varying expectations as to the function of the unit and the school's need to re-accept children after attendance. The HMI survey found that the time children spent in the units varied from two months to seven years, with children formally suspended accounting for about a quarter of the numbers in the units visited.

In common with all other special provisions, procedures for arranging the admission of children are better developed than procedures for returning children to their appropriate schools. The reasons for this are obvious: teachers in the original school become accustomed to the absence of a troublesome member of the class and are reluctant to contemplate the child's return. Children, in their turn, become settled and accustomed to working in a smaller group with, perhaps, more sympathetic teaching approaches, and are themselves reluctant to return to a situation where they were in so much trouble. They may even become difficult to avoid such a return. Children often perceive themselves as having failed in their ordinary schools and may be un-willing to re-visit a situation in which they have had this experience. Attendance at the unit may have been preceded by a good deal of unhappiness for both the child and his parents: the latter may not want to see their children return to a situation which caused them so much difficulty.

For all these reasons full-time units are particularly liable to fill up, and once they have filled up cause problems within the schools because of 'lack of provision'. Such a progression is not really necessary, and this is best demonstrated by a specific example. The ILEA Finsbury Unit was established after an educational psychologist had identified a group of pupils, mainly in their second or third year at secondary school, who appeared to lack a personalised internal structure. It was hypothesised that these children had not been exposed to sufficiently good models of structure in their early childhood to allow them to internalise models of control on which to base their later behaviour.

The unit was organised in three levels of structure to cope with this hypothesised lack of structure within the children:

— 'formal structured': a class in which the pupils were told exactly what to do and how to do it;
— 'informal structured': a class in which activities like art, debating or cookery could take place, but in which the children could have some say in what they should do, within a set of formalised and practical rules;
— 'informal unstructured': a class in which the children were able

to decide what to do and how to do it with the support and
guidance of adults.

The purpose of this carefully designed structured progression was to
enable the deliberately identified and specified children to accept help,
advice and support and to internalise the controls so that they could
work independently without coming into continual conflict with the
ordinary school system. A three-week initial trial period was instituted
as part of the assessment-for-admission procedure, so that there could be
very little margin for error in accepting children for the full programme.
This, together with the well-defined justification underpinning the unit
and the detailed provisions made to satisfy this reasoning, have
resulted in an adjustment programme which has been able to help
children in a totally different fashion from the large majority of off-
site units. It does not deal primarily with undifferentiated problems
arising from child/school conflicts, but with clearly defined problems
which can be treated in a specific and certain manner within a system
which *requires* eventual re-attendance at school.

The Main Provision

Despite the increase in the range of special provision it is quite certain
that the large majority of the children who cause problems will remain
in the classrooms of ordinary schools. These are the main provision: it
follows that they are also the main solution if any is to be found.

The Warnock Report (1978) made recommendations which would
increase the pressure on ordinary schools to integrate children with a
large variety of handicaps. Berger *et al.* (1977) have reported on one way,
using techniques of behaviour modification, that teachers may be
assisted in coping with and preventing the problems of difficult
behaviour in school. Many other researchers have commented upon the
need to assist teachers in understanding the child both as a determiner
of his own problems and in terms of the interaction between the
teacher and the child. The value of such approaches is obvious and has
led, in one way or another, to child-centred provisions within the
schools which have been of great benefit: counselling systems and the
organisation of pastoral systems which attempt to offer each child the
opportunity to relate to caring adults.

Admirable though these approaches are, they beg one important
question: the role of the school in creating the problems it sets out to

solve. Rutter *et al.* (1979) and Galloway and Goodwin (1979) have shown very clearly how the school affects the behaviour and achievements of children and how significant are inter-school differences. Although almost a part of folklore, until recently there have been few studies which have *demonstrated* the extent and effectiveness of school organisations upon their pupils. Very little work, as a result, has been done in attempting to modify school organisation to take recognition of this fact. Such a recognition may well help us to make what might be a quantum leap, not just in ways of helping children in difficulty but of avoiding the *creation* of problem children.

Until now, most treatment and provision has been predicated upon the basis of locating a fault or an area of blame in an individual. While this might be either child or teacher (in practice, rarely the latter), provision has usually been made on the assumption that removal of the child into some sort of treatment unit is the correct approach. Even the meticulous work of Boxall (1976) and Mycroft (1978) has been based upon this premise: that it is the child and his attitudes which require adjustment and that the special provision should be organised to effect this change.

If the work of Rutter and others is to carry through into practice, a fundamental change in orientation is required. Concentration upon individuals inevitably results in the erection of systems which replicate the doubtful provision of the past—doubtful in theory and practice. Concentration on the analysis of the school which throws up a lot of children with behaviour problems would seem, on the basis of recent research, to be a more realistic reaction—and a more professionally satisfying one—than trying to locate the blame in an individual child. Such a concentration requires no formal structure, no formal organisation and no formal provision. What it does require is a continual emphasis and awareness on the part of teachers, administrators, educational psychologists and advisers as to the importance of school organisation in the life of the child and the role that this organisation plays in the creation of problem behaviour. An emphasis of this type accepts the fact that schools are complex organisations, akin in many dynamic respects to a small village—which many of them approach in size. In a village there is a complex social dynamic, underpinned by an understanding of the social structure, an awareness of the rules that govern interpersonal behaviour and of the effect of the various levels and functions, that the inhabitants use in their day-to-day roles and relationships. In this way, schools resemble villages; in another way they resemble large, and not very well organised, factories. In a factory of, say, two thousand workers (pupils), a hundred charge-hands (teachers), twenty foremen (senior staff) and two or three directors (head and deputies), it would be astonishing to find a work force that would accept a system in which each worker was engaged on seven or eight different pieces of work each day, for several different charge-hands in seven or eight different workplaces, to seven or eight different standards. This, effectively, is what occurs in many secondary schools under conditions which often would not meet accepted trade union requirements.

If these two analogies are acceptable and the influence of the school in creating its own difficulties is also accepted, then the role played by the social organisation of the institution in the behaviour difficulties manifested by some children becomes obvious. Similarly, the ineffectiveness of traditional solutions (simply removing the child from one place to another) has also to be accepted. Children's problems need to be seen in the context of their working day and the people they have to relate to.

In many schools children are expected to cover quite large distances in what almost amounts to negative time. One lesson begins at 10 a.m., for example, while the other ends at 10 a.m., but little allowance is made for pupils who arrive 'late'. And the teacher who arrives late for the same reason may start off with a disruptive class who have been kept waiting. Different kinds of lesson activities can interact with each other. Physical education is often found to precede lessons in which there is a high incidence of problem behaviour. The reason for this is not just that children find it difficult to accept ordinary classroom constraints after the freedom of physical expression, but also that P.E. teachers are often more likely than other staff to be able to 'put down' pupils who are troublesome. Any resentment of this may be vented on the next teacher, particularly if he is young and inexperienced, the lesson unpopular and towards the end of a tiring day.

A lunch-time shared by all the children in a large school is noisy, bustling, confusing and can lead to difficulties between children, which then become pressures to be vented in the classroom. Lack of understanding of the lines of authority within a school can lead to exploratory behaviour by pupils. If the lines of authority are not clear, new teachers will be tested, through deliberate behaviour, to see if they know as much as the children do of the organisation of the school. Teachers vary not only in their experience. The difficulty of adapting to different teaching styles and the differing 'languages' of particular subjects, and the need to discern an individual teacher's style and expectation can also lead to exploratory behaviour with, occasionally, explosive results.

This list of problem-creating situations could be continued almost indefinitely. There is little use in attempting an exhaustive list, assuming it were possible; what matters is the perspective for understanding that the examples signify. Taking an attitude which accepts that the school plays a part – often a major part – in the difficulties it has to solve means that teachers, psychologists and others concerned need to consider how the school system can be modified to minimise the problems themselves. The effects of this type of intervention, orientated away from the palliative provision of displacement units, could be a reduced dependence on outside agencies and special teaching in schools that function more happily and more successfully.

Some of the effects in a variety of schools in which this approach has been tried have been as follows:

(1)   The institution of a five-minute break between lessons with correspondingly sharper penalties for late arrival. The effect of this has been to give children a chance to chat – which they need to do – as well as to collect books and materials in an unhurried way so that they arrive at their subsequent classes unflustered and ready to begin work.

(2)   The publication of clear and comprehensible handbooks which explain the school's functioning in precise detail for children, staff and parents so that they all work by the same rules. This type of specification reduces the kind of behaviour noted earlier – testing out by children of teachers and by teachers of the organisation.

(3)   The reorganisation of the timetable so that the effects of traditionally difficult lessons, e.g. maths with low-achievement groups, are minimised by distributing them evenly throughout the week and avoiding double periods. Changing the time of day and, when this is not possible, ensuring that the teacher involved is not young and inexperienced are other elements in this juggling with the circumstances that can combine to produce problems.

(4)   The careful introduction of new children to the school through a first year organised in larger teaching sessions with a small number of teachers, so that children become familiar with, and part of, the system that is to house them for the subsequent four years, without immediately losing the kind of supportive context which characterised their much smaller primary schools. The effect of this has been a smooth junior/secondary transition,

almost eliminating the near-traumatic effects experienced by some children at secondary transfer.

(5) The establishment of systematic alternatives to the usual teacher responses to disruptive behaviour by the provision of 'referral rooms' to which a child can transfer immediately to continue working under the eye of a 'powerful' teacher. The most successful of these comprise a room, deliberately quiet, in which a child works at the appropriate subject, returning to his class and normal timetable at the end of the period. Children who are sent to the referral room are followed up, through counselling or tutoring, if they are referred more than a given number of times; a similar check is possible on teachers, if they seem to be referring more often than expected.

This type of approach is obviously neither as simple nor as quick in apparent effect as transfer to an on or off-site unit, where reactions to problem behaviour cannot only be seen, but be seen to be done. Disposal is a simple 'solution' which threatens nobody; change, reconsideration and re-evaluation in a sense threatens everyone it touches. For this reason it always involves a process of exposition, consultation and the monitoring of progress. The main initiative always has to be within the school although the educational psychologist can guide the discussion and analysis of the problems the school is facing. The effects and benefits of this kind of analysis are many, not least the feeling that the school is competent to cope with its own problems from within its own resources. Teachers' feelings of being de-skilled, of feeling that there is somebody else better qualified to deal with children, are diminished. Teacher confidence is crucial: it is unreasonable to expect them to display caring and considerate attitudes towards children in a situation which predisposes the production of problems.

However, a functional analysis of schools will not eradicate the needs of children who require specific help with some learning and emotional difficulties. It cannot replace what Berger (1976) calls 'special forms of competence' in teachers if the diverse needs of children are to be met. It is though, one way, not yet fully explored, of avoiding 'the artificial by-product of contemporary institutions, created and reinforced by them in pursuit of their short-term ends' (Illich 1971): the creation of more and more units to deal, in an undifferentiated way, with children whose problems are partly created by the schools on whose rolls they appear.

Special placement solutions to problem behaviour create the need for elaborate structures, rules for admission, discharge, education and conduct. As such they are expensive, cumbersome to administer, and no more than palliative. They only deal with *created* problems, which is why their success must be limited: they do not help to *avoid* problems. Only system change can be truly preventive: compared with the existing range of solutions it is, in the end, simply much more efficient.

6 TREATMENT UNDER ATTACK

Norman Tutt

In 1978 there were over 100,000 children in the care of local authorities in England and Wales. The vast majority of these children were in placements provided, managed or monitored by local authority social services departments. The number of children in care of the local authorities has grown consistently throughout the past decade despite the fact that the numbers of children actually entering care have dropped each year. The increase can only be due to children staying longer in care than previously thereby leading to a building up of the total. Table 6.1 illustrates the trend over a seven year period following the implementation of the Children and Young Persons' Act (1969).

Table 6.1: Children in Care (England and Wales) on 31 March 1972-8 (thousands)

1972	1973	1974	1975	1976	1977	1978
90.6	93.2	95.9	99.1	100.6	101.2	100.7

Source: DHSS, *Children in Care in England and Wales, March 1978.*

Children can be received into care at any age and can if necessary remain in care until their eighteenth birthday or, in exceptional cases, their nineteenth birthday. However, the age distribution of children actually in care shows that the largest proportion (46 per cent) are of secondary school age, and that a majority (65 per cent) are within the age limits of statutory education (see Table 6.2).

Children may stay in care for substantial periods of their lives, although their length of stay will obviously vary according to the reasons for admission. It is important to remember that the majority of children (69 per cent) are received into care at the request of their parents under Section 1 of the Children's Act (1948). Many of them are expected to stay only a short time while some family crisis, which necessitated their admission, is resolved and following which they should return home. Despite this, as Table 6.3 shows, over 77 per cent of the children have been in care continuously for more than a year. These figures show that a substantial number, approximately 75,000, are spending the greater part of their formative years in state care.

Table 6.2: Ages of Children in Care on 31 March 1978

Age	Percentage
Over 17 years	1
16-17 years	23
10-15 years	46
5-9 years	19
1-4 years	10
Under 1 year	1

Source: DHSS, *Children in Care in England and Wales, March 1978.*

Table 6.3: Children in Care on 31 March 1978

Duration of most recent care episode[a]	Percentage[b]	Number
5 years and over	27	27,000
3 years but under 5 years	17	15,000
1 year but under 3 years	33	33,000
6 months but under 1 year	10	11,000
8 weeks but under 6 months	8	8,000
Under 8 weeks	6	6,000

Note: [a]A care episode is defined as that period in which a child is continuously in the care of a local authority without a change in his legal status.
[b]Percentages do not add to up 100 because of rounding.
Source: DHSS, *Children in Care in England and Wales, March 1978.*

It would be wrong to assume that all of the children in local authority care need 'treatment'; for the majority such a concept is inappropriate. The children are in need of substitute care as an alternative, or supplement, to that provided by their own family — because of temporary disruption of the family structure, e.g. mother's confinement, or because of features which are likely to prove more permanent, e.g. breakdown of parents' marriage. The primary responsibility of the local authority social services department to these children is to provide care. In doing so they may uncover a range of treatment needs for the children which it would be impossible to neglect. Many of these needs will not have been identified or remedied by the child's family and will be straightforward health or developmental problems, e.g. dental caries, hearing impairments or speech impediments. A number of others may reflect emotional or behavioural problems, e.g. enuresis, violent outbursts. Obviously any responsible state agency would feel obliged to take remedial action on these problems once identified, even though they were not the prime reason for referral.

More important for this discussion is the group of young people who are placed into the care of local authorities *primarily* for treatment. These children, who are a minority of the care population (12 per cent), are placed in care by the juvenile court, having been found guilty of a criminal offence. Another small group (approximately 1000 in 1978) find themselves in care by the same means although their behaviour is not defined as criminal, e.g. non-school attendance. This chapter is specifically concerned with looking critically at the theory and practice underlying the concept of residential treatment for those children whose behaviour causes them to be defined as delinquent.

'Soft Option' or 'Capitalist Indoctrination'?

The attack on the treatment philosophy is interesting, since because it comes from so many diverse sources it may prove irresistible. The various arguments for and against treatment can be caricatured as:

(1)   On one side treatment is attacked because it is seen as a soft
       option and expensive. Those who choose this stance believe
       that the state has the right to punish – if necessary, physically –
       those young people who 'attack society' (News report, 17 May
       1979). Moreover, many believe that this is what the young
       person expects and understands. Indeed the 'child's right to
       punishment' is the dictum adopted by one advocate (see Tutt
       1975). The proponents call for the re-introduction of corporal
       punishment, often with a misleading fervour which suggests it
       may have actually gone, whereas the evidence is that it is still
       widely used in schools. They believe, instead of 'mollycoddling'
       treatment, 'a short sharp shock' will bring the young bully to
       his senses. The short sharp shock can be provided in an
       economic, utilitarian regime in which the offender is denied
       comforts, kept active and made to work harder. These
       attackers reject the thought that it costs £30,000 to provide a
       place in secure accommodation, and £25,000 per annum per
       child to use it. They regard this as unnecessary nonsense: the
       child could be kept locked up merely by 'turning a key in a

door'. The concentration on high staffing ratios and professionally qualified staff is regarded by them as the irrelevant
protectionism of a quasi-profession.

(2)   On the other side the argument is advanced that deviancy *per se*
does not exist but is the definition that those who control the
power structures of society put on the behaviour of a substantial
number of the working class. They point out that since violent
behaviour is the expected norm amongst working-class
adolescents, then there is nothing abnormal or deviant about
it when considered within the social context in which it arises
(Mungham and Pearson 1967; Pearson 1976). Therefore, to
treat the violent or thieving individual is no better than
indoctrination, since it is merely imposing the standards of
the ruling elite on to the working class. It is not done for the
benefit of the individual but merely to pacify him and remove
him as a threat to the ruling structures. This, of course, explains
why the prisons and community homes are full of residents
drawn from particular classes within society. Their needs are
not best met by treatment by professionals who make a fat
living out of the process, but by cash-benefit schemes which
would alleviate their financial problems.

Why Treatment Doesn't Work

The treatment philosophy is attacked by practitioners in various ways.
Those with a research view may point to the fact that there is no 'cure'
for delinquency because it is produced by a number of socio-economic
factors which the treater can not affect (Tutt 1974; Cornish and Clarke
1975). Placing the young offender in care may lead to the alleviation of
some of the personal problems of the young person so that he is better
adjusted, but that does not mean he will remain non-delinquent when
returned to his own community with its inherent pressures. Cornish
and Clarke, in their controlled study of a treatment regime compared
with a traditional regime, could find no statistically significant difference
in the outcome behaviour as measured by further offences committed
by boys who had experienced the different regimes.

Alternatively, it has been argued that treatment is not currently
working because it has not been given the opportunity to work. It is
estimated that about 15 per cent of child care staff are professionally
qualified and of these many have only the basic qualification. Staff turnover is high, as is illustrated by a survey conducted by one Children's
Regional Planning Committee which showed that 30 per cent of

residential staff in Community Homes with Education changed their
posts in one year (London Boroughs Regional Planning Committee's
Report 1979). At the same time, salaries and capital investment have
been low. In other words, residential establishments have never been
given the resources to carry out treatment and are now condemned
because they are not effective.

All of these viewpoints have a certain amount of validity as a selected
sample of the evidence indicates. One of the most powerful arguments
against the effectiveness of treatment approaches to delinquency is the
fact that treatment and non-treatment settings seem to have little effect
on the re-conviction rates of young people discharged. Research has
made the public familiar with the distressingly low success-rates of any
institution which is expected to reduce delinquent behaviour. A range
of methods operating in a range of institutions produce surprisingly
similar results for groups of the same age and history of previous con-
victions. This is true whether they be closed Borstals (81 per cent of
15 to 17-year-olds re-convicted within two years after release), Junior
Detention Centres (70 per cent of 14 to 17-year-olds re-convicted within
two years after release – Home Office 1979), or secure units within the
community homes system provided by the local authorities (76 per cent
of boys re-convicted within two years after discharge – Millham *et al.*
1978). It is currently not possible to produce similar figures for the
open Community Homes with Education. However, as Millham (1975)
pointed out in his study of approved schools – the predecessors of
Community Homes with Education – although schools varied in their
outcome, overall the average 'success' rate was over 50 per cent re-
convicted within two years of release. The failure to halt offending
behaviour is important; and the present writer has suggested that there
may be no treatment for delinquency:

> The words chosen are 'reacting to' rather than 'caring for' or 'treat-
> ment of' delinquents . . . because it is becoming increasingly more
> difficult to maintain a belief in the 'treatment' of delinquents. By
> that I mean a process which ensures that a child who is classified as a
> delinquent before a treatment phase is not classified as such post-
> treatment. In other words delinquents who are treated are not re-
> convicted (Tutt 1978).

If this view were to become widely accepted it must have serious
implications for both policy and practice, since both are currently based
on the belief that offending behaviour can be treated. Thus the

argument runs: this child has offended, therefore the state can compulsorily intervene – not because we want to punish him, or incarcerate him in order that he can not do it again – but in order to treat him so that he will not need to offend in future and therefore be rehabilitated to the community. Our failure to be able to carry out this treatment must pose a strain on the logical argument underlying current policy.

The logic of treatment intervention is even clearer, but more suspect, when the action taken against non-school attenders is examined. In 1977 in England and Wales there were 1801 actions taken against children for non-school attendance; 1036 of these resulted in a care order (Personal communication: DHSS 1977). The majority, if not all of these orders, will have led to the removal of the child from home. Will this action have guaranteed the child attended school and received adequate education – presumably the justification for the action? The answer is 'no'. The chances are that the child in England will go to a local observation and assessment centre which will produce an assessment and indicate possible future placements. The assessment centre will probably have about 30 children resident. These may well range from very young children who are at risk of non-accidental injury by their parents, to 16-year-olds awaiting court appearances. The 30 children of wide age and ability ranges may share three teachers who have to contend with a floating population and have little contact with the child's previous school to allow continuity of reading schemes, etc. After assessment there may well be difficulty in placing the child and he could stay at the centre for an extensive period. Assuming he is 'placed' this may well mean that he is returned home or fostered; the only treatment he will have received for his non-school attendance being a further fracture in the continuity of his education. If he is placed in a children's home to attend a different outside school, he suffers the same discontinuity with the addition of a further illogicality, namely that since his problem was school attendance, in some respects it can only be achieved within the existing educational framework. But to achieve that, the child had had to be removed from his home and provided with substitute care. If he progresses to a Community Home with Education, there is no guarantee that he will receive education in any way connected with his previous school experience or geared to his possible future (HMI 1980).

The irrationality of the observation and assessment process has been discussed fully by the present writer (Tutt 1976, 1977), who points out:

Assumptions underlying current philosophy of observation and

assessment centres are: (a) that human behaviour is constant . . .
(b) that children in care have idiosyncratic problems open to
remedial intervention . . . (c) that the observation and assessment
centre is functional.

Developments in research, as well as practice, tend to suggest that all
three assumptions are invalid.

(a) A child in a different situation is a different child; i.e. the child in
a residential O & A centre is, by definition, not manifesting the
problems he has in adjusting to his school or home environment. If this
is so, then assessment needs to concentrate on specific questions; for
example, instead of saying 'this is an aggressive child', we need to ask
'with whom is he aggressive, how often, in what situation, and in what
way?'

(b) Children in care have idiosyncratic problems open to intervention
. . . West and Farrington's (1973) longitudinal study of over 400 eight-
year-olds in London showed quite clearly that the five major factors
linked with delinquency are:

— low family income,
— large family size,
— having a parent with a criminal record,
— having parents considered to be unsatisfactory in rearing children,
— comparatively low intelligence.

These factors emerge from nearly all the research in this area of child
care. It is significant that of these factors only one is idiosyncratic to
the child, namely that of low intelligence. Thus four of the five major
factors are not individual to the child and can not, therefore, be rectified
by isolating the child, assessing him, and then applying some form of
remedial action. It should also be obvious that any remedial intervention
directed at the child must be doomed to failure if the child is then
returned to an unchanged hostile environment which still retains the
major criminogenic factors. If this argument is accepted, serious doubt
must be thrown on the validity of the second assumption underlying
our current observation and assessment policy.

(c) The O & A centre is functional in that it is able to allocate children
efficiently to appropriate placements . . . There are two basic grounds
on which to question this assumption: first, on control of resources, and
secondly, on the practical possibility of having sufficient knowledge for
the task. Observation and assessment centres are unable to allocate

children efficiently quite simply because they have no control over the forward placement of children. If forward placements such as fostering, intermediate treatment, and home on trial are added to the (residential) possibilities, the range becomes so wide that it is unrealistic to expect the observation and assessment centre to have sufficient knowledge to allocate rationally. The assumption that these centres are functionally effective in terms of an allocation machine is therefore questionable.

One more reference to non-school attendance worth considering is the disturbing case chronicled by Sutton (1978) in the *Howard League Journal.* He describes the case of a five and a-half-year-old son of a single parent, who was failing to attend school regularly. The educational welfare officer initiated court proceedings but by the time these took place the boy's attendance was 100 per cent. Despite that, the child was removed from home for assessment. The outcome was to place the boy back in his own home and school only after considerable emotional trauma for the child and his mother, and enormous costs to the community.

If the argument against the treatment of delinquency and allied behaviour problems proves to be so overwhelming, what process can replace it, given that the community feels compelled to do something about disruptive and disorderly children? Is the answer punishment, as some would suggest, or are there realistic alternatives? I believe there are.

Changing the System is Easier than Changing the Individual

Prevention

Clearly it is in the interests of both the child and the community to prevent delinquent behaviour and the subsequent reaction by society. However, it would be unwise to advocate the traditional preventive strategy based on early identification of children 'at risk' and consequent action from the state agencies. Unwise, since there is no evidence that such a strategy would work; in fact there are indications from sociological studies on labelling that any process of selection would identify more children at risk than would otherwise become delinquent. To take a simple example, it is known that a disproportionate number of delinquents come from broken homes. However, it is also known that many children from broken homes do not become delinquent. Consequently, if children were to be identified as potential delinquents on the basis of whether or not they came from broken homes, too many would be identified. This remains true even if complicated correlations and collations of numbers of factors are made. West and Farrington (1973) using data on five family-background characteristics collected before the boys in their sample were aged 10, in a longitudinal follow-up study correctly identified 31 boys who were convicted of offences before the age of seventeen, but incorrectly labelled 32, and 53 delinquents were missed completely out of a total sample of some 400 plus.

Even if children could be identified accurately and placed in delinquency-prevention programmes, little progress would be achieved. Firstly, we do not know what action is preventive. Most such programmes are normally geared to compensatory education or more general 'enriching' experiences for deprived children. Both approaches may be of value and benefit the child but do not have any proven influence on future delinquent behaviour. Moreover, such early identification may actually help create delinquent behaviour by labelling the child, grouping him with other delinquents and thereby giving him a self-identity as a 'problem' which he then lives up to. Under the general heading of prevention, it would seem more realistic to advocate a series of preventive strategies aimed at reducing criminal *opportunities* and not the presumed future delinquent behaviour of individuals. The Home Office Research Unit in one of their publications, *Crime as Opportunity* (Mayhew *et al.* 1975), give a number of examples where the opportunity for delinquent behaviour appears to stimulate such behaviour. Removal of the opportunity reduces the behaviour. For example, the wide-scale introduction of steering locks on cars reduces the opportunity for car theft and therefore the amount of illegal driving and taking away. The use of lighting and vandal-proof materials reduces the number of thefts from telephone kiosks. The work by the planner Oscar Newman (1972) on 'defensible space' in architecture may mean that housing schemes can be designed in such a way as to reduce vandalism and theft of property by allowing individuals identifiable areas for which they are responsible and 'defend'.

Changes in operational services may have an impact beyond that expected; for example, the 'truancy sweeps' operated by the juvenile bureau in various divisions of the Metropolitan Police. Young people obviously below the age of sixteen on the streets during school hours were stopped and questioned by patrolling officers. Their stories were checked with parents or teachers and, if necessary, they were returned to school or home. In one division this action coincided with a reduction of 26 per cent in reported auto-crimes, i.e. theft from cars as well as theft of cars, and a reduction of 36 per cent in petty crimes of theft (Metropolitan Police Juvenile Bureau Statistics 1979). The responsible reaction of a particular industry may have similar effects. The retail industry, concerned by the high level of loss from shops, running at 2 to 3 per cent of turnover and accounting for some £650 millions of losses, has set up its own association to encourage local High Street stores to co-ordinate their approach to shoplifting. This is particularly significant since most of the retail chains involved have traditionally been competitors. The association claim (APTS Newsletter 1979) that in a campaign in one South London shopping area prior to Christmas, they were able to reduce predicted losses from stores by increased security, staff activity and publicity. This increased activity led to substantially more prosecutions, initially, of those found stealing from shops, of whom half were under seventeen years of age. The association also claims that once the message went round the youth sub-culture in the schools that the stores were 'clamping down', the number of young people attempting to shoplift dropped rapidly.

These approaches reverse the traditional argument that criminal behaviour springs from within the individual who will require specialist help to stop the behaviour. Instead they imply that delinquent behaviour is the result of the interaction of the individual with his environment and that the state and other agencies have as much responsibility to eliminate those factors in the environment which are criminogenic as to intervene in the individual's life.

The Schools' Role

So far the major force for the prevention of delinquency among young people has only been referred to incidentally – and yet must be the most potent since it has access to all young people consistently over many years. This is the school-system which has always seen itself as involved in fostering responsible attitides and standards of behaviour through teaching 'moral education', 'citizenship' and the like. There is now growing evidence to suggest that the schools should actively reconsider their role in the prevention of anti-social and delinquent behaviour since they appear to be almost uniquely effective. Even taking intake variables into account, schools vary markedly with respect to pupils' behaviour, attendance, exam success and delinquency. In short, even in disadvantaged areas, schools can do much to encourage desirable attitudes and attainments. As Rutter (1979) and his team conclude: there is 'a greater effect of schools on children than children on schools'. These findings are not dissimilar to those of

Millham *et al.* (1978) in their study of approved schools, who found that variations in outcome in terms of re-conviction for offences, although small, could be related to the 'regime' of the approved school.

All of these findings suggest that not only could schools be managed and operated in such a way as to reduce delinquency amongst the intake and thereby be positively preventive, but by the converse, badly managed and operated schools may actually encourage delinquency.

Alternative Strategies for Young Offenders

Preventive measures will, it is hoped, reduce the number of young people committing offences, but what of the minority who continue to offend and, therefore, presumably require some form of state intervention? What form and intensity should this take? Given the evidence of the failure of intervention reviewed in this chapter, should we not be thinking in terms of scaling down the levels of compulsory state involvement?

There has been a strong feeling for some time that young people who offend may not best be helped by the judicial process. Scotland has, of course, led the world in setting up a non-judicial system of children's hearings to help young people in trouble (see Bruce 1978). This feeling has been given the backing of research respectability by the work of West and Farrington (1977), who in their longitudinal study of some 400 young men growing up in South London, found that adolescents matched on self-reported delinquency had different rates of offending depending on whether or not they had appeared before court. In other words, an appearance before a juvenile court did not *reduce* but in fact *increased* the possibility of further offending. It would be wrong to assume any causal link between the events but it does suggest that a court appearance may not have the salutary effect it is assumed to possess. There are now a number of schemes beginning to develop which aim at diverting the young offender from the juvenile court. The most impressive of these in terms of its widespread effect is not in fact called a diversionary scheme but is the police cautioning system operating in England and Wales, whereby a young offender usually on his first or second offence is issued with an official caution by a senior uniformed officer. In 1977 51.7 per cent of young offenders under the age of seventeen charged with an indictable crime were dealt with in this way, so that it has now become the most common disposal for young offenders. It may actually be quite successful. The Metropolitan Police followed up all cautions made on young people in 1976 for two years. Of those cautioned 71 per cent were in no further trouble (Metropolitan Police Juvenile Bureau Statistics 1979). This does not prove conclusively the success of cautioning; it may merely show how few first offenders re-offend. It has been argued that cautioning, far from diverting young people from the courts, has in fact inflated the crime figures by recording a number of children and their offences which previously would have been dismissed by the police (Morris 1978).

A caution involves only limited intervention with a potential offender. A number of police forces, dissatisfied with this, are establishing their own juvenile-support schemes, in which a member of the juvenile bureau acts as a supervisor to the young person and his family. In some areas, e.g. Cheshire, the police in conjunction with the Social Services Department have drawn up a panel of volunteer 'aunts and uncles' who befriend a young person after a caution and offer him adult interest and guidance. In other areas the police have established links with social services departments running intermediate treatment schemes and, after the child has been cautioned, he will be given a chance to become involved in such schemes. As this is voluntary, the child's passage to the social services department does not necessarily have to involve the police. A pilot scheme in the West Midlands has been set up between the intermediate treatment officer of the local Social Services Department and the manager of the local branch of Woolworths. Until recently Woolworths had a firm policy that all shop-lifters caught were to be prosecuted. Now the manager is prepared to waive prosecution of juveniles as long as they are willing to be visited by the intermediate treatment officer and discuss with him the possibility of taking part voluntarily in one of the schemes. This is clearly a radical diversionary programme.

More interesting is the trend for juvenile courts to use short-term disposals, such as a fine, attendance centre or conditional discharge in preference to those disposals which preface a long-term state intervention. Short-term disposals have increased as shown in Table 6.4. The trend may well reflect disillusionment by the magistrates of social services (work) departments. But it also reflects part of the community's belief in natural justice that the level of intervention should somehow be linked with the seriousness of the offence, and that what are fairly trivial offences do not merit intensive intervention in the life of the child and his family. This reaction is similar to that reported by Tulkens (1979) who, in trying to explain the differences in prison

Table 6.4: Males (10-17 years) Convicted of Indictable Offences
(percentages of total disposals for the age group)

	1967	1970	1977
Attendance centres	8%	9%	11%
Fines	30%	32%	35%
Conditional discharges	21%	20%	23%
Borstal and detention centres	3%	4%	8%

Source: Home Office, *Criminal Statistics for England and Wales 1978.*
Contrast these figures with 'treatment' disposals (Table 6.5).

Table 6.5: Treatment Disposals

	1967	1970	1977
Supervision by a social worker	26%	24%	17%
Care order or equivalent	8%	9%	6%

Source: Home Office, *Criminal Statistics for England and Wales 1978.*

population between the Netherlands and United Kingdom – i.e. 20 per
100,000 inhabitants compared with 75 per 100,000 in the UK – points
to a change in attitude of the Public Prosecutor. 'Five years ago the
policy was: to prosecute unless prosecution was not required in the
public interest. Now, however, it is: do not prosecute unless required
in the public interest.' He argues that this attitude has led to a marked
decrease in the number of prison sentences with no notable switch to
alternatives.

It is therefore possible to identify some clear moves or shifts in
policies and organisations for dealing with juvenile offending and related
behaviour problems. These shifts have important implications for the
educational services whether mainstream schools, special schools, special
units, or advisory staff such as educational psychologists. These shifts are
first, that the primary 'defence' against delinquency is a more active
preventive strategy and that recent evidence will produce strong pressure
on the schools to take a major role in this strategy. Pressure will be
exerted to make schools responsible and accountable not only for
academic achievement, but for the socialisation of the children entering
the schools. The management of schools will be expected to adopt
policies to ensure that they do not increase behaviour problems among
their intake and, more positively, to take active steps to reduce its appearance.

Secondly, if the schools fail to avoid delinquency they will not be able to expect ready relief from their problems by the courts sending the child away for long-term 'treatment'. The cumulative effect of the movements outlined in this chapter will be for young people who offend to be retained in the community, and that means continuing to attend their own schools with some additional support provided by a professional social worker or, more likely in the future, a volunteer adult who is interested in young people and prepared to commit time and effort in befriending an individual. If a child's offences are sufficiently serious to merit being 'sent away' by the court, the chances are that the intervention will be fairly short and the child then returned to the community. The shortness of the intervention, between six weeks and one year with the median well towards the shorter end of the range, will mean that schools will be faced with receiving back young people, for possibly two more years of education, who have experienced vastly different sets of institutional controls and relationships than the majority of their peers. This problem already arises with junior detention centres to which a boy can be sent at 14 years of age; with remission he would normally be only six weeks in the detention centre and then be returned to his own school. The experience of a detention centre run by the Prison Department and staffed by prison officers will vividly colour his views on control and authority figures as well as radically affect his self-image. Schools will find themselves having to cope with the predictable problems of re-adjustment as well as trying to liaise with social services departments and Home Office establishments in order to provide some continuity in the child's education.

Experiences of this kind will force schools to reassess and, if necessary, modify their internal organisation; it will also mean that education authorities will have to give serious consideration as to how they meet their responsibilities to, and for, difficult and disruptive children. Finally, it will mean that the support and advisory services will be under pressure to produce guidance for teachers on such issues as control, discipline and how to manage and avoid violent confrontations in the classroom.

7 WITHDRAWAL UNITS AND THE PSYCHOLOGY OF PROBLEM BEHAVIOUR

Robert Daines

The range of 'withdrawal' provision, its characteristics and alternatives, was reviewed in Chapter 5. The present chapter recapitulates some of these themes but mainly explores the concepts of 'problem behaviour' that they exemplify.

The development of 'withdrawal units' has been idiosyncratic and piecemeal: they did not form a coherent national development but were established to meet the perceived local needs of a school or education authority. By 1976, and as a consequence of their considerable growth in the early seventies, such units began to attract some attention. Topping and Quelch produced a small survey in that year and Her Majesty's Inspectorate and the Schools Council initiated studies that were published in 1978. The national picture drawn by these surveys is a highly varied one but despite this, some important general principles and implications emerge.

Units demonstrate every conceivable variation in finance and organisation. They may be located on a school campus or housed in separate premises. They may serve one school or several. The HMI survey found that the latter case applies in two-thirds of the units which draw from between two and ten schools. They noted that one, two and three-teacher units each account for approximately a third of the total. The number of pupils varies considerably, a pattern further complicated by the part-time nature of some attendance. The typical unit has two teachers for between 12 and 16 pupils. The Schools Council Project team observe that larger units, with two or three teachers, were on the whole 'more successful' than one-teacher units. They add that the ideal group size is between eight and twelve. Above and below this range they detect problems of 'group cohesion'. Both major surveys agree on the high qualifications and wide experience of unit staff. The HMI survey reports the average length of service as eleven and a-half years.

For whom are units intended? One unit may be designed to provide for 'non-attenders'; others for 'school phobics', 'disrupts', 'aggressive and violent pupils' or those who are 'emotionally disturbed'. Even units which have a special remit to consider all children with 'behaviour problems' find these categories relevant. However, a 'school phobic' is also a 'non-attender'; an emotionally withdrawn pupil may be a 'school refuser'; a 'disrupt' may also absent himself from school; he may or may not be 'aggressive and violent'. Clearly, instead of taking these categories at face value, a survey must ask questions to establish which classifications most generally apply. HMI observe that most pupils are in units because of disruptive behaviour in the classroom and that for a quarter of them this had led to suspension from school. They also find that many have long histories of non-attendance; that over half of them are in their 4th and 5th years; and that the majority can be described as 'low achievers' or 'remedial pupils'. A very similar picture is drawn by the Schools Council Project team.

All that the survey data so far tells us, besides indicating certain years and ability bands, is that units contain pupils who have adopted certain roles in relation to the school-system. In general terms it is difficult to proceed beyond this point in characterising the children in withdrawal units. The Schools Council report refers to 'emotionally disturbed' and 'conduct disordered' pupils but fails to clarify or define these terms. HMI comment that the problems that had resulted in particular pupils being referred to units were 'extremely complex'. They distinguish between two groups: those experiencing acute difficulties arising out of transient crises, and those with chronic problems of adjustment and/or serious social and family breakdown. In both surveys, and with no examination, inadequacies in homes, neighbourhoods or children are used to explain pupils' behaviour in school. These observations stand uncomfortably alongside the data which show that children in units can most easily be characterised in terms of their school life – i.e. as 4th or 5th years or as 'academically poor'. There is little direct research evidence that helps to fill out the picture. Lane (1976) looked in detail at the 'most' disruptive and unmanageable boys drawn from a school population of 10,000. He confirmed that 'poor achievers' were disproportionally represented: 20 per cent were 'non-readers', while a further 40 per cent were still in the process of mastering basic written English. At a more interpretive level, Lane also found, using Eysenck's (1952) personality dimensions, that there were personality differences between his selected group and 'normal' students. The former tended to be more 'toughminded' and 'extravert'. Lane relates these observations to difficulties in getting such pupils to accept rules and constraints, to their hostility to adults and their concern with immediate reward.

How the behaviour of unit pupils is understood and interpreted is reflected in the philosophies and practices of the units. This brings us to the further question of their function. HMI note that a few are seen as punitive institutions. Pupils work hard on tasks which are not primarily selected for their curricular relevance, and are closely supervised during every part of their school day. The operating principle of these units is that placement is undesirable and that in order to avoid this outcome pupils will be motivated to control their behaviour. Unit staff are forced to play an unpleasant and unrewarding role if this *modus operandi* is to be effective. Such units are almost exclusively 'on site' and serve only one school. In the vast majority of cases a more positive approach is taken, however. The reasons for the pupils' behaviour are explored, or projected, and the work of the unit then organised in these terms. According to the Schools Council team, 90 per cent of the teachers see their main purpose as helping pupils with social and emotional problems. This aim has its practical expression in social skills training, education for personal relationships and various types of counselling. HMI comment on the wide range of aims and philosophies to be found in units. These observations tie in with the conventional picture of pupils' problems that presuppose causal inadequacies in families, neighbourhoods and the children themselves.

With regard to the nature of the educational provision itself the pattern is more uniform. HMI remark that whatever the emphasis, teachers overwhelmingly stress the need for pupils to develop systematic patterns of working. They find that 46 per cent of units place a major emphasis on remedial work and add – not surprisingly – 'this seemed to reflect the belief that low achievement can lead to disruptive behaviour'. Similarly the Schools Council team find that more than half the units include educational progress as part of their main purpose. They stress that the 'most successful' ones have carefully planned programmes to develop good working habits and intensive remedial help to ensure competence in the basic skills. The singular nature of unit educational programmes appears to be a better guide to their 'undoubted success' than the diversity of their other aims and practices.

Observed changes in pupil behaviour, between school and unit, are used as the criteria for success by both surveys. They are impressed by the 'good working atmosphere' generally found and the absence of the type of incident that marks the disrupt's behaviour in school. HMI report 83 per cent as the average attendance figure, which indicates a much improved situation. This is confirmed by the Schools Council team. However, one major theme in the role and function of units is set to confound this satisfactory picture.

Given their budgets, staffing and facilities, withdrawal units cannot be expected to provide their pupils with a complete educational programme. They differ from the special schools in being planned on the basis of part-time and/or short-term attendance. Both surveys note that most units have as their principal aim *the return of the pupils to normal schooling.* Despite this, periods of stay were said to vary from two terms to seven years! In the case of off-site units serving several schools, a form of alternative education has often developed by default. This is particularly true for the large number of disaffected 14 to 16-year-olds. In view of their age and the technical difficulties of fitting into the complex curricular patterns at this stage, few of these pupils are likely to see school again, so teachers are faced with the difficult choice of either looking ahead to the world of further education and uncertain prospects for employment, or directing their efforts towards returning pupils to school.

But there are important differences between regarding units as alternative education for 4th and 5th-year pupils and viewing them as rehabilitation centres for secondary pupils regardless of age. The criteria for success clearly change. Successful adjustment to the unit only applies where it is recognised as a 'no return' alternative form of schooling. If the aim is to return the pupil to ordinary school then successful adjustment there, following re-integration, is the appropriate criterion.

There is a third possible model. This involves 'supporting' a pupil while he continues to attend school, a role already played by some part-time units. In the 'sanctuary' or 'home base', the pupil spends a certain amount of time each week in the close company of a sympathetic teacher; hopefully, he comes to like and respect him. As well as being in a position to communicate school values, the teacher can begin to make his interest conditional on the pupil's good behaviour and provide an incentive for regular attendance. In order to work effectively this model is necessarily restricted to single-school, on-site units. The unit must be bound up with the values and events of a particular school's life and be suitably placed to monitor the pupil's behaviour. The model also presumes that the child can sustain a personal response. In spite of its current popularity the rationale of the rehabilitation model is decidedly weak. Short-term placements only make sense if the problem behaviour is related to either temporary social circumstances or easily remediable characteristics of the child. Examples of the former would include stresses caused by the break-up of a family or the onset of a handicapping condition. For the latter, we have to consider the 'treatment' programmes of the units. There are three main emphases (and mixtures of them).

By carefully manipulating a pupil's circumstances, particularly in terms of what he finds rewarding, old habits and behaviours can be broken down and new ones built up. The techniques involved travel under the label of behaviour modification. But the circumstances of the pupil's problem behaviour are a school, not a unit, phenomenon. Successful adjustment to the unit, in as much as it results from employing these techniques, cannot ensure re-adjustment to school. There is every likelihood that a return to former situations will lead to a return to former behaviour. It may be possible to transfer some of the 'new circumstances' along with the pupil; apart from being of limited scope, however, this transfer depends on the unit having a powerful voice within the school's pastoral-care system.

Another approach uses the influence gained through developing a personal relationship with a pupil. By making his expectations clear, a teacher can alter the student's behaviour, and the longer the time he spends with a particular teacher, as in the home-based model, the wider the teacher's influence. Return to school is a return to different, and various, teachers with varying expectations of him. The third approach is a development of the second. The pupil's relationship with the teacher facilitates conversation about attitudes and experiences. Counselling techniques are based on this model. They depend on the existence of numerous subtle connections between thought and behaviour. Though the likely success of such techniques is theoretically very difficult to evaluate, some relevant empirical evidence has been collected. Wolff (1976), in reviewing the literature on anti-social behaviour, has found that there is little evidence that it can be modified using such means. Lane observed that his 'disruptive' group responded to utilitarian rewards rather than counselling and linked this, plausibly, with his earlier observations on their personalities.

Unit educational programmes stand up better to close examination. They tackle problems that are central to school life and are thus working towards the successful re-integration of the pupil. The educational deficits of academically poor and remedial students can easily lead to frustration and failure. Under the regime of the subject timetable they can find themselves pursuing low priority tasks of impossible accomplishment – e.g. learning French when they can barely read and write English, or studying physics when simple multiplication still presents problems. They are more likely to discover that they cannot carry out assignments or that rote copying is the only way to complete them.

The pupil's behaviour in school must be related to his experiences of school life. Despite its comparatively poor resources a unit has distinct advantages over a school as an educational placement. Given its small pupil/teacher ratio and its flexible organisation, it can offer an individually tailored curriculum and a great deal more pupil-directed teaching. The absence of the frustrations and failures of school may well be a factor in the numerous examples of successful adjustment to units. For some pupils, return to school, with improved literacy and numeracy skills, may change their experiences of school life to the extent that the problem behaviour fails to reappear. Although in this form the notion of the unit as a 'rehabilitation centre' has some substance, the role is appropriate for only some of the children referred.

Does the problem behaviour disappear in units because their circumstances are different from those of the school? This possibility has been raised in a number of contexts. Units can offer specific techniques for managing pupils' behaviour, influential personal relations, to the same end, and relevant and sensitive teaching. Other advantageous changes include the absence of organisational demands, such as finding correct rooms for particular lessons, and removal from the inappropriate expectations of teachers and peer group. These differences between schools and units mean that the latter are in a better position to ensure that pupils pursue educational activities under the guidance of experienced and able staff.

That unit teachers are of a high calibre is confirmed by both the major surveys. The Schools Council team observe that the general principles of 'treatment' in successful units were the caring attitudes of teachers, control through explicit rules and consistent expectations, allied to the judicious use of approval and success. They note that academic work was often very structured and add that 'this reflected the view that pupils in the unit work better and feel more secure within a tightly structured programme'. HMI suggest that a factor contributing to the good attendance record was the small size of the units which 'enabled close personal relationships between teachers and pupils'. Flexibility of organisation and working patterns and less-complex academic demands were also held to be beneficial influences. In summary, both surveys found that 'circumstantial' factors were of paramount importance in securing the successful adjustment of the pupil. This point is generally recognised by the staff of referring schools. How often have they been heard to say 'he needs more individual attention and supervision'?

Testimony also comes from the children's own behaviour. HMI comment that though pupils often become good attenders in part-time units, their attendance at school remains poor. If pupils' adjustment is relative only to their changed circumstances then the notion of units as rehabilitation centres fails to have any substance. Despite this, both surveys found that a large majority of units aim to return pupils to school, re-integration being considered appropriate *when a child's behaviour ceases to present problems to unit staff.* HMI note that regular assessment and constant observation are the usual means of assessing the possibility of a return to normal schooling.

But when a pupil is returned to school, not only does he lose his close relationship with a teacher, but also a compact familiar environment and standards of a particular order, for the school and unit invariably have different ones. He also loses a certain consistency in treatment – i.e. two teachers can be more consistent than sixty-two – and an educational programme far more individually tailored than anything the school can offer. Therefore, to any positive statement on a unit report – e.g. 'he has learned how to control his temper, relate to his peers, organise his own work, or relate and respond to teachers' – must be added the qualification *'in the unit'.* However able and well intentioned the staff, there remains an inconsistency between the knowledge that they can work with a certain pupil and the confidence that as a consequence he will be able to adapt to school life again.

In an informal survey by the author (Daines 1979) carried out in two northern counties, it was found that problem behaviour re-appeared in over 60 per cent of re-integrated pupils. The classic pattern seemed to be that its re-appearance followed an initial, six or seven-week period of successful adjustment. This is consistent with the view that a return to the original circumstances will eventually lead to the re-emergence of the original problem behaviour. Even the policy of gradually re-integrating pupils over a period of weeks fails to tackle the issue. Both major surveys bypass the question of re-integration. HMI states that 'the percentage of pupils who returned to school was difficult to calculate'. They make no attempt to evaluate the success of the policy. The only problems they project are those created by the reputations of the pupil and unit, leading to negative expectations; and those concerned with the technicalities of curriculum adjustment.

Successful integrations do occur. We have already discussed the possibility that the notion of rehabilitation may have some substance for academically poor children who are given intensive remedial teaching. The criteria by which they are deemed ready for school have little to do with their social behaviour in the unit. By developing literacy and numeracy skills, unit staff hope to remove the frustrations and failures of school life. If the intervention aims at changing problem behaviour by approaching it through an educational programme, then the role of the unit is akin to that of a conventional remedial department. Even those changed circumstances that lead to better management of the pupil in the unit have usually been features of remedial departments – i.e. small groups, a close relationship with a teacher, and so on. The only difference is that units make a more conscious adaptation to the problem of managing the pupil. For example, they are more likely to use specific behaviour-modification techniques, and when pupils attend part time, their withdrawal from lessons is often linked to the requirement to contain their behaviour. If the problems are related to the child's educational competence then the criteria for re-integration has to be in these terms, and a judgement made to the effect that the pupil can now 'cope' in school: in essence that he can now manage a subject timetable. This criterion is identical to that used by the remedial department. However, if the pupil is re-integrated, on the basis of his behaviour in the unit, into an unchanged school setting, there is a greatly increased chance that the problem behaviour will re-appear. The fact that a pupil 'settles down' in a unit, attends regularly and engages in the required educational activities may be, in itself, largely irrelevant to the question of whether he should be re-integrated. None the less this is the general form of criteria employed for return to school.

Unit pupils can most easily be characterised in terms of their school life, and the success of withdrawal units can best be understood by viewing them as educational placements. If the problem exhibited in schools later prove to be largely manageable in educational terms, then can we be confident that schools are meeting their obligations to pupils? What, if anything, does the success of units tell us about the failure of schools? Though units are in a better position than schools to educate certain pupils, cannot mainstream schools emulate their circumstances? Does every big comprehensive have a group of pupils that necessarily require the services of a unit? Does every school need a 'sanctuary', 'remedial' and 4th and 5th-year unit? No school has all three types and many have none. To what extent are units picking up problems that are the schools' responsibility?

What clearly emerges from studying the operation of withdrawal units is that problem behaviour in school is best understood in terms of school characteristics. However actually or apparently justified, there are dangers in construing it in terms of personal and social inadequacies. Such a view overlooks the fact that the behaviour occurs in school and usually exclusively in school. As we have seen, the circumstances surrounding the behaviour are a factor in determining it – and changing it. Failure to appreciate this can mean that units adopt complex programmes and interventions that are difficult to evaluate, i.e. education for personal relationships, social skills training and counselling. The point is not that these are ill conceived or unnecessary, but that they are secondary. The work of a unit needs to be primarily organised in terms of the factors in the immediate situation in which the behaviour occurs. There is considerable evidence that these 'primary' interventions are successful in eliminating the problem behaviour whether it be disruption or non-attendance. If units are succeeding in manipulating the 'primary' school factors then it is vital that we scrutinise these same variables within schools to see if the behaviour problems referred to units can be tackled at source.

A first question is: how do schools view problem behaviour? In examining this we meet the same distinction between social and personal definitions and school ones. Where the main emphasis is placed seems to be related to the dynamism or lethargy of the 'construing' school's system. To the extent that a school is reluctant to change and adapt in response to the needs of its intake, it will be inclined, in order to defend itself, to locate problems in external causes. Thus pupils' behaviour is seen to spring eternal from social and personal factors. Along with the one surveying units, Her Majesty's Inspectors prepared a separate report that discussed truancy and behavioural problems in schools (HMI 1978a). They found that where schools successfully manage disruption and non-attendance, difficult behaviour is defined in terms of school factors. Their central point is that 'schools should accept the fullest responsibility for coping with *their* problems'. HMI note that discipline depends on mutual respect between pupils and staff and that the desire to maintain good relationships with the teachers is a powerful incentive for many pupils to behave acceptably. They stress 'the need to offer relevance and success to students as a means of avoiding behaviour and attendance problems', and observe that *'if you want something to happen in a large organisation you must structure it to happen'*.

In pursuing the question of the school's responsibility for problem behaviour it is useful to distinguish between those children who lack basic educational skills and those who have little aptitude for a conventional skill curriculum. The former can be defined as those whose level of literacy and numeracy are such that they find it difficult to cope with a subject timetable. For them the educational activities are both of a low priority and difficult to execute. Remedial pupils can more easily encounter frustration, failure, mechanical tasks and inappropriate and unintersting activities. It is common to underestimate what a history of failure to gain a reasonable literacy-level means to pupils. There is nothing more true generally of schools than the requirement to read, write and spell, and nothing more likely to lead to widespread rejection than failure to learn them. Usually 'remedial' pupils are only withdrawn from certain lessons. It may well be that the large percentage of such pupils in units indicates that the referring schools are failing to give them appropriate and relevant education. In the informal study, previously mentioned, eight out of ten pupils were judged by their unit teachers to be 'unable to cope with subject teaching and to be in need of full-time literacy education'. *None* had been receiving this in their referring schools.

There are a large number of children referred to units who, although basically literate and numerate, find much of the school curriculum inappropriate, irrelevant and uninteresting. Raven (1979) has recently completed a major study into the attitudes of secondary school pupils and their teachers. He has found that roughly a third of pupils sometimes or always hate going to school. More than half of them consider that over 50 per cent of their school subjects are 'boring and useless'. Raven comments that 'so great is the disenchantment that it is difficult to see how teachers can achieve any goal effectively'. He notes that there is a reciprocal attitude on the part of the teachers. The majority defined less academic pupils as 'lazy, disruptive, uninterested, incapable of learning and no good at anything'. From Hargreaves (1967) and Power (1969) we know what a significant factor, in fostering anti-social behaviour, teachers' expectations are.

In their study of attendance and behaviour in secondary schools, HMI note that 'absence rates support the view that much of the provision for the less academic student is missing its mark'. They suggest that some truancy may be attributable to poor and unimaginative teaching which fails to recognise the changed interests and attitudes of adolescents. Ravens' most significant finding is that pupil disenchantment is strongly related to expectations of their future social destination, i.e. job, career interests, etc. He comments that 'if pupils don't like schools it is because they cannot see the relevance of what they are doing there'. In this event we should expect the level of 'disenchantment' to increase markedly as pupils progress through the school with concommitant effects on attendance and disruptive behaviour. HMI noted, in their survey of units, that over half the pupils are 4th and 5th years; Galloway (1976) found that 4th-year absence rates were nearly double those of the 3rd year and that this doubling process was repeated again in the 5th year. In their other study of attendance and behaviour in secondary schools, HMI observe that all schools reported a recognisable and steady increase in unauthorised absence from the 3rd year onwards. They add that 'in some areas truancy in the 5th year presented almost intractable problems', and provide a direct link with 'pupil disenchantment' when they comment that 'for some pupils motivation diminishes rapidly from the 3rd year onwards, particularly for those with a poor level of achievement and low aspirations'.

Given the current picture of much secondary schooling, and the nature of unit success, it seems that the provision of a unit can easily become an alternative to tackling serious problems within the school. Before a unit is created, the scale and nature of the problem behaviours at issue need to be carefully examined. In this process a first step is to define the problems in terms of school variables. In the past this has frequently not been the case. The HMI survey found that many units were housed in very poor conditions with low budgets. They appeared to be a 'scratch' provision following on from the need to withdraw pupils rather than the projection of a constructive educational environment.

Topping and Quelch, in their 1976 survey, obtained information from twenty local authorities. They found that only a small number had made any attempt to assess the incidence of the problem before setting up units. There were nearly as many different aims reported as authorities replying; these were often ill defined and confused aims. Few stated concrete aims in such a way as to make it possible to determine whether or not they had been achieved. Very few authorities had clear-cut criteria for admission and there was little agreement about the technique needed to change behaviour. The procedures for discharge were even less clear than the vague criteria for admission. These points, taken in conjunction with observations on the high quality of unit staff (confirmed by HMI and the Schools Council team) led Topping and Quelch to conclude that dedicated staff are left to wrestle with the problems of running units that are ill conceived and inadequately provided for. Experienced teachers have been attracted to units by the prospect of being able to put into effect practices and philosophies that are difficult to develop in the ordinary school. In saying this our picture of the 'ordinary school' must be informed by our earlier discussion.

Would tackling problem behaviour at source eliminate the need for withdrawal units? We have already noted the fundamental differences between units and schools. Their cohesiveness and small size, their good pupil/teacher ratio, and their ability to isolate a pupil from the behaviour-maintaining expectations of others, are difficult to emulate in the large comprehensive. It could be that some pupils may only be manageable by maximising the circumstances that units can offer. If the pupils' background problems are temporary ones then the notion of units as short-term placements is appropriate; if their problems relate to a need for remedial teaching, then the same consideration applies. Where the background problems are long term – and this may be due to the long-term failure of the school – then units either function as alternative provision or provide a 'home base' for the child throughout his school life.

In attempting to answer the question whether or not schools can manage problem behaviour without devising units, we can do no better than quote the HMI truancy report. They cite the example of four schools in 'poor' areas with 'difficult' intakes, who have succeeded in managing their problems. All placed the major emphasis on setting consistent, attainable and appropriate educational objectives for their pupils. Of these schools, one established a unit but closed it after eighteen months; a second closed theirs after only three weeks; the staff of a third didn't feel that there was a need for a unit, of any type, and a fourth had a unit but this functioned as an integral part of the remedial department.

8 ONE SCHOOL'S EXPERIENCE

John Hastings

It would be idle of me to pretend that the organisational change within
a school to be described in this chapter was done with much knowledge
of what is presented in other parts of this book. Certainly among the
staff of the school there were few, if any, with a theoretical background
in the field. What I hope to demonstrate is that organisational change
within our school (and presumably the same arguments will apply to
other institutions) has altered the pattern of opportunity for deviant
behaviour. This is what we sought to do. We made no statistical measure
of the problems of the behaviour which occur out of the classrooms
as they existed before the changes. We were aware that the problems
existed and there was a consensus of opinion that they were on the
increase. Equally, we cannot formally demonstrate that the changed
pattern has reduced the problem. Those who had to deal with the
problems know they have decreased and it is perhaps of great
significance that the caretaker and cleaning staff have approached me
to ask that we stay with the new arrangements. Their job is significantly
easier, not only because they can start work earlier, but because the
school is cleaner and less vandalised. For a group who have worked in
the school for a long time not to hanker after the 'good old days' speaks
well of the change. Educationally I cannot say with any certainty that
there has been change other than that I am aware of an improvement in
attitude, usually called 'tone', which can be seen as an educational
improvement. Measured only on the level of a boost in staff morale
because the job has been made a little easier, without any fall in
efficiency or responsibility, the exercise was worth doing. Few will
disagree that the better the morale the better the educational provision.

The Start

Over the last twenty years teachers, experienced and raw beginners alike,
have become increasingly aware of the narrowing of the line between the
maintaining of control and the complete loss of the opportunity to
teach. As this has happened in the more guided atmosphere of the classroom, so the difficulties of the less organised areas of supervision, the

general supervision of play areas during breaks and lunch hours, have caused more worry, in some cases bordering on fear. The seemingly hopeless task of preventing vandalism in the form of graffiti, litter, the defacing of work and other displays, and bullying and intimidation, is a constant worry for teachers.

More worrying, particularly for the conscientious, is the difficulty in following up any action taken against those who indulge in misdemeanours and the imposing of sanctions in the general supervision periods. The lack of information a teacher has about the majority of pupils is such a barrier to efficient control that there is a tendency to let standards slide, to turn a blind eye on the very occasions when action is demanded. The more observant teachers see the periods of non-classroom supervision as the periods when serious confrontations are the most likely. These are the times when pupils are demonstrating their individual power to their peer group; when there is general noise and bustle; when the teacher meets pupils he does not know, whose habits of speech he is unaware of, whose 'normal' demeanour is not accepted because it is not recognised as such; and when the pupils are aware that the exercise of authority by the teacher is difficult.

All schools have these problems to a greater or lesser extent. Our school had. We used the common daily organisational pattern of a 15-minute morning break, a one and a-quarter-hour lunch time, and a 10-minute afternoon break. The morning was made up of a half-hour assembly and group period plus four teaching periods of 35 minutes. The afternoon had a 5-minute registration period and four 35-minute periods.

The school building is twenty-five years old, brick built and with no social areas. Boys' and girls' toilet and cloakroom facilities are at opposite ends of the school. Break-times during bad weather are, therefore, particularly unpleasant, tiring and difficult. During a period of continuous bad weather in the Autumn of 1976 we decided to try abolishing afternoon break for a time. There were the expected cries of no time for pupils to use the toilets; no time for staff relaxation; no break to refresh the pupils' minds. But after a fortnight without the afternoon break there was no desire to go back to the old system. The abolition of the task of general break supervision was seen as a most acceptable advantage but it was also found that there was no disruption caused by excessive visits to the toilets, and that pupils during the last two periods of the afternoon showed no additional fatigue. In fact, it was generally agreed that the last afternoon session was improved as less time was needed to settle the pupils following the freedom of a break. A move to abolish morning break was soon quashed as it was agreed that the morning session, in effect five periods, was too long to go without a break.

In summary, the abolition of the afternoon break had increased staff morale by halving break-time supervision and it appeared to have marginally increased efficiency by not having a session of settling down following playground freedom. It had certainly removed one period when vandalism and bullying could, and sometimes did, occur. The limited but apparent success of the change led us to look seriously at the lunch-time problem. Of 760 pupils, about 300 stayed at school for a cooked lunch, up to 200 stayed and brought their own sandwiches, and the rest either went home or visited the local shops. The school rules suggested that only 5th-year pupils should leave the premises if they stayed for school lunch or sandwiches, but the campus is too large and has too many exits for the rule to be maintained. Pupils leaving the school campus at this time created the attendant problems. Many of them just wandered the streets; there was always the possibility of petty theft; smoking took place in public; noise and litter could not be contained within school bounds and this caused concern to local residents who, in many cases, were elderly. Added to this, afternoon truancy is more likely if there is time to get some distance away from the school at lunchtime. The temptation to stay away is greater.

Those who stayed on the premises had little to do. Clubs and societies existed but giving pupils the opportunity to attend was not easy as the school meals service could provide one serving point only and this meant that to ensure fairness a system of rotation was in operation. Any such system causes conflict if some pupils are allowed to queue-jump for particular reasons, and this is aggravated when a club activity crosses the year boundaries. Priority lunch arrangements, though possible, were unpopular with both pupils and supervisory staff. Lunch hours in bad weather were periods of high incidence of damage, not necessarily deliberate but caused by high spirits and boredom. Occasional outbreaks of malicious damage took place at lunchtime when supervision was at its minimum level and the building difficult to 'police' – the connotations of this term are significant.

A simple reduction of the lunch break was not possible. School meals were still being served about a quarter hour before the end of the lunch hour and shortening might have led to more pupils requiring lunch – a self defeating move. Senior staff felt that something must be done to shorten the period of non-activity for pupils and a decision was made to attempt to modify the timetable to allow partial overlap of teaching time and lunch time. The following tentative timetable was put to a staff conference in October 1977:

	Years 1 and 2	*Years 3, 4 and 5*
8.55-9.05	Registration	Registration
9.05-9.30	Group Periods or Assembly	
9.30-10.05	Lesson 1	Lesson 1
10.05-10.40	Lesson 2	Lesson 2
10.40-10.50	Break	Break
10.50-11.25	Lesson 3	Lesson 3
11.25-12.00	Lesson 4	Lesson 4
12.00-12.35	Lunch	Lesson 5
12.35-12.45	Changeover time	
12.45-1.20	Lesson 5	Lunch
1.20-1.55	Lesson 6	Lesson 6
1.55-2.30	Lesson 7	Lesson 7
2.30-3.05	Lesson 8	Lesson 8

There was some criticism of the short morning break and there was a move to have the assembly and Group-period time timetabled as lessons for one day a week for years 1 and 2, and two days a week for years 3, 4 and 5. For these reasons the suggested timetable was modified and because many staff preferred that arrangements of lessons should allow as many double periods as possible for the upper school, and as we had link courses with the local Further Education College four-periods long, the version below was used for further consultations.

	Years 1 and 2	*Years 3, 4 and 5*
8.50-9.00	Registration	Registration
9.00-9.30	Lesson, Group Periods or Assembly	
9.30-10.05	Lesson 1	Lesson 1
10.05-10.40	Lesson 2	Lesson 2
10.40-10.55	Break	Break
10.55-11.30	Lesson 3	Lesson 3
11.30-12.05	Lesson 4	Lesson 4
12.05-12.40	Lesson 5	Lunch
12.40-12.50	Changeover period	
12.50-1.25	Lunch	Lesson 5
1.25-2.00	Lesson 6	Lesson 6
2.00-2.35	Lesson 7	Lesson 7
2.35-3.10	Lesson 8	Lesson 8

Part of the thinking behind the arrangements, particularly the grouping of the years and the ten-minute gap was:

(1) Analysis of the number of pupils staying for school lunch showed that there was a falling-off in the senior school, with a corresponding increase in the incidence of sandwich eaters, and it appeared that the school meals service would find a more equal distribution of numbers by such an arrangement. It would have been possible to split a year but we hoped to avoid this if we could.

(2) Counts showed that the number of children likely to require meals during one sitting could be served in 25-30 minutes but this meant the last pupils served at 12.35 would not have time to eat in reasonable comfort without the ten-minute period in between lunch services.

The first hurdle, staff acceptance, was achieved, albeit with some misgivings about digestions and the ability of the pupils to settle and concentrate without a longer break. No evidence either to support or to contend this was available but enquiries of local firms who had shortened lunch breaks, in many cases to 30 minutes, revealed no evident reduction in efficiency. It was gratifying that the staff as a whole accepted the increase in the school day when compared with the original draft version.

The timetable for further necessary consultation and implementation was agreed as follows:

(1) School meals service – as soon as possible;
(2) Governing body – November 1977;
(3) Education authority – as soon as possible;
(4) Parent and pupil body – March 1978;
(5) Start – September 1978.

The School Meals Service

This body, both school and central, were most supportive and whilst recognising the possibility of an increase in meals required, saw no difficulty in coping. They welcomed the opportunity to treat the meals as two separate events, creating menus and quantities suitable to the ages and inclinations of the pupils. They were willing to work to a tighter service schedule and faster hatch service.

The Governing Body

The Governors accepted the arguments in favour of the changes. They showed some concern over the earlier arrival home of pupils in the afternoon, but were quite prepared to accept that half an hour at a loose end at lunchtime was less desirable than an extra half hour in the evening as it had been established that most pupils would be able to get into their homes. The Governors asked for a trial period of one term but were persuaded that a timetable constructed for a period of one term only was wasteful of effort and in the end agreed to a period of trial of one year. In the event, a period of one term's trial would not have created difficulty because of the way the construction of the timetable was ultimately approached.

The Education Authority

The authority saw no legal difficulties but made the following observations:

(1)   Morning breaks should on no account be less than fifteen minutes as the time for social contact between staff was minimal under the new arrangements. They believed that casual interchange of information between staff is vital to their morale.

(2)   Full consultation with parents must take place.

The Parent Body

Informal consultation with pupils had been made throughout the period the scheme had been considered and we expected parents to be very much influenced by the pupils' opinions in any case. Consultation was done in two stages. First a letter describing the scheme and calling a meeting was distributed to all parents. The meeting was attended by representatives of approximately 80 families and by the very nature of such meetings, those present were, in the majority, those who were opposed to the changes. Arguments put against the scheme were:

(1)   Given that they would have time to get home, pupils who had brothers and sisters in the two halves with different timetables could not come home to a meal together. This argument could not be refuted.

(2)   The whole scheme was arranged to make life easier for the teachers and was an easy answer to the restrictions on lunchtime supervision imposed by the teacher unions. It was pointed out that the original concept of the change was

originated well before the 1978 sanctions were imposed.
Parents could see, and accepted, that the proposed scheme
would make lunchtime supervision much easier and more
effective and that sanctions, if imposed again, would not have
the catastrophic effect they had earlier in that year when
pupils had to be denied school meals. Most parents accepted
that the headteacher's responsibility for the safety and welfare
of pupils would be more likely to be satisfactorily carried out
with an arrangement similar to the one proposed.

(3)   Some parents thought that there would be little time for the
food to be digested. It was pointed out that the majority of
pupils did not give themselves such time in any case. Many
spent their free time after a gulped meal dashing about playing
football or other active games, using the library and joining
in other extra curricular activities.

(4)   Others expressed a worry that the extra-curricular activities
would suffer. The effect in this area was difficult to predict.
Present difficulties were described and it was thought by some
parents that, given the willing participation of the staff, clubs
and societies after school would benefit from the fact that
only the enthusiasts would join and therefore the quality of
the activities would be enhanced.

(5)   Many parents pointed out that many pupils who went home
for lunch would be unable to do so following the change
because of shortage of time. This was agreed but it was demonstrated that the total available time for lunch provision was
longer under the proposed arrangements than under existing
arrangements and therefore more would be able to stay for a
cooked lunch. Moreover, the fact that the lunch hour was
divided meant that the facilities for those eating packed lunch
could be used twice and thus more than double the existing
number could be accommodated.

(6)   One mother stated that in her home lunch was regarded as a
family event and she would be bitterly disappointed if the
family meal was broken by a change in school arrangements.
The school could only sympathise with her view and show
some disappointment that it was not well supported.

(7)   Some parents suggested that the matter was in any case a *fait
accompli* and that I was merely going through the motions of
consultation. At this point I suggested I would hold a
referendum of all families and only if a substantial majority

were in favour of the change would I carry it through. I also gave an undertaking that should the new arrangements prove inoperable, or show signs of adversely affecting the education of the pupils, I would abandon it and revert to the existing timing of the school day.

This satisfied the meeting and the parents present agreed they would follow the majority decision.

The Referendum

This was a simple questionnaire asking a straightforward 'yes' or 'no' to the scheme and, very importantly, as a major increase in numbers staying for school dinners would have caused insurmountable difficulties, how many pupils in the family would stay for school dinner if the change was made. An all out effort was made to ensure the return of ballot forms and a 97 per cent return was achieved.

The result was a vote in favour of the change of slightly greater than 2 to 1, 68 per cent to 32 per cent of the returns, and the predicted numbers for dining purposes could be managed. The majority seemed to me to be adequate and the decision to go ahead was made.

The Implementation

Once this decision had been taken, we had to begin work on the revised timetable. The first stage was to make an analysis of the additional constraints created by the new system. The most obvious trap to avoid was that of timetabling an individual member of the teaching staff to be teaching both fifth periods for the two groups, otherwise there would be no lunch time for that teacher! We also accepted that it would be undesirable to have a double period in one subject split by the lunch break. This meant that single periods had to be, and were, accepted by all departments. We had to ensure that the new timing of the school day did not make it impossible for the local Further Education College to accept the link course students. Fortunately the College was willing to accept the link course pupils for either the morning or afternoon sessions. The afternoon session was preferable for the school as pupils could have an early lunch and, to allow for travelling time, could continue beyond 3.10 p.m. Morning sessions would not be quite so easy as pupils would have difficulty in travelling from the College and also eating their lunch in time for the beginning of the afternoon session.

Lastly, to ensure that the promise made to the parents that we would revert to the old times if there was any difficulty, we decided that a timetable should not be created which would need a total rewrite if it proved necessary to abandon the scheme. We hit on the simple device of constructing a timetable for a continuous eight-period day. This could then be separated at the points appropriate to the year group and the lunch period inserted. This method of approach meant that it would be impossible for an individual member of staff to be timetabled for both lunch periods. It would also mean that if the timetable needed to revert to similar lunch times for all the school it could be pushed together again and opened out at the same point for all year groups. The only requirement to satisfy both contingencies was that for years 1 and 2, periods 5 and 6 had to be single periods. The timetable proved to be of little extra difficulty than had been our normal experience.

Dining arrangements were reasonably straightforward. Traditionally, 5th-year pupils had always gone straight in to lunch from lessons. This privilege we decided to continue. In the first week the 4th year would follow the 5th and the 3rd year follow the 4th. The following week 3rd year would follow the 5th and 4th year follow the 3rd. The position of the 3rd and 4th would then alternate weekly. In the second sitting the 2nd and 1st years would alternate weekly being first in the queue.

Supervision would be required in three places – the queueing area, the dining room and the playgrounds. The queueing area would need supervision during the first half of a sitting and the play areas only during the last half of each sitting. Supervision of the dining area would be covered by staff taking a school lunch and completed by the welfare assistants transferring from the queue duty to the dining area once the queue was dispersed. The short lunch break caused us to accept that staff duties should be minimal. Staff volunteering for duty would be asked to help collect the money and register free meals (meals are served on a cafeteria, pay-as-you-collect-your-meal system) and their period of duty would be 15 minutes, two members of staff covering each sitting. The queue and playground supervision would be covered by a rota of the headmaster and deputies. General supervision duties were expected to be lighter as fewer children would be 'free' at any given time. Sandwiches are eaten in the foyer and the corridor adjacent to the dining hall, and supervision of the pupils eating sandwiches falls within the purview of the queue supervisors.

Evaluation

As I write this chapter the scheme has been in operation for a year and
it is possible to judge the effects, advantages and disadvantages, both
expected and not anticipated. First, we must look at the objectives and
see if they have been realised. Initially, the exercise was simply to cut
down on the opportunity for deviant behaviour and reduce the period
of supervision of the pupils necessary during the lunch time.

The very nature of the change achieves the second of the objectives.
In the absence of statistical measures whether or not the first has been
achieved must be largely a matter of subjective judgement. As previously
mentioned there has been less litter (less time in which to create it?),
the school has been cleaner (fewer people moving in and out?) and
there has been a negligible amount of vandalism (less time for boredom
and greater awareness by the smaller groups of pupils of the presence
of supervision?).

The year has contained more than the usual amount of bad weather
and under past arrangements snow and inclement weather would have
created problems during the whole of the spring term. As it happened
the majority of pupils were either waiting for dinner or dining under
some supervision and the lack of social areas was much less noticeable.
During the teacher sanctions the school meal arrangements went ahead
uninterrupted and this was a major bonus. Most headteachers will say
that there are more problems of indiscipline and attendance following
a period of sanctions and particularly the withdrawal of teachers from
lunch-time supervision. We noticed little change in attitude and
behaviour compared with the problems induced by the 1978 period of
sanctions.

During the year there have been no complaints from local residents.
In the past the school has always had several complaints about noise,
litter, vandalism and insolence. Relationships with the neighbourhood
now appear to be better.

The separation of the seniors and juniors during the short time
available for lunchtime play has meant that the groups have been able
to play their peer-group games without interference from the other
groups and the consequent irritation with each other which usually leads
to incidents of bullying and occasional fights. There has been less of the
inter-year rivalries than usually experienced and the 1st year pupils have
found settling down into the school a little easier.

One of the early worries was that the groups not being taught would
interfere with the concentration of those still in the classroom. Such

interference has been much less than expected and occurs only in the teaching spaces bordering directly on to the playground. The feeling of the staff is that as more teachers are engaged in activities about the school, because of their work, they are exercising an unorganised super-vision. They are rarely called upon to take any action but their presence is an advantage in maintaining a high standard of unobtrusive supervision. The worst period of interference is when the 1st and 2nd-year pupils disperse to their first afternoon lesson. At this time the 3rd, 4th and 5th year are usually in the middle of a double period lesson.

Registration is an adversely affected afternoon activity. Prior to the new arrangements there had been a five-minute registration period at the beginning of afternoon school. In many ways this was a time-wasting activity with pupils having to go to their group rooms and thence to their classroom – the whole school moving twice within five minutes – but it did ensure accurate registration. The split timing does not allow for such arrangements as group teachers may well be engaged in teaching other groups and the rooms for registration of some groups may be in use for teaching purposes. The arrangement under the new system is for registration slips to be sent to the office and the details transferred to registers. This is a time-consuming occupation for the clerical staff, and an easily forgotten procedure for the teaching staff. The answer to the problem could be to have a registration period at the end of afternoon school: an efficient, but not legal, procedure.

At the parent consultation meeting the parents thought the long wait for lunch for the 1st and 2nd-year pupils would be too much for them to bear. This has not proved to be so. Creatures of habit as they are, they soon settled to the system. Under the previous system, because of the four-year rotation, the time for taking lunch could vary from week to week by as much as 45 minutes. The variation has been reduced to under 20 minutes and digestive systems seem to be the better for it!

The most serious adverse effect on the staff has been the reduced opportunity for informal teacher-to-teacher contact. A number of teachers had come to rely on the lunch break for seeing colleagues on matters of departmental policy, pastoral matters, discipline and so on. The short lunch break means less time for discussion and the staggered timetabling means that individual teachers may not be free at the same time. It is, of course, true to say that there is not the same rush to get off the premises after afternoon school, and some contact is possible then, but equally the inherently early leaver still has the same urge. Formal meetings of various staff groups have been more readily accepted as they can now be completed before the rush-hour traffic starts, but this does not entirely compensate for the loss of time for informal contact.

The extra-curricular activities have been affected in a mixed way. There is no doubt that those of the pupils who do stay are enthusiastic but this has reduced their number and may well have lost those who, in the past, joined in for the wrong reasons, but having joined found a genuine interest and developed an enthusiasm for the activity. Formal activities such as the drama productions and musical activities gain much because rehearsals can be arranged to take place before the light fails and before evening activities of the pupils become a serious deterrent to attendance. Games activities have benefited from the change in that practices can take place in light conditions and without the slowness caused by following too closely after a generous portion of pudding. Pupils can leave for away matches at other schools without having to miss lesson time. On the other hand, there is sometimes a long wait for the arrival of a visiting team. Some teachers have not started clubs and activities because they felt there might be a change in policy after a year and that activities started in after-school hours might have to close if the school reverted to the previous school hours. Now that the pattern seems to be settled I expect more activity to be initiated in after-school hours.

The change has created more time for the pupils between the end of afternoon school and the time for paper rounds, errand boy work and other part-time employment which impinge upon the time the pupils expect to be able to use for social activities. Consequently there is less excuse for non-completion of homework tasks which can now be completed before other activities. The problem of securing the work is not so easily solved; time available has, in some cases, nothing to do with the refusal or unwillingness to complete homework tasks. There has been some talk of arranging a supervised area for homework to be done in school during the hour after school closes.

Public examination did not cause an unsurmountable problem. Examining boards agreed to the school starting their examinations much earlier in the afternoon and, if necessary, examinations went on after school. The proximity of the school hall to the dining hall meant that on some occasions extra supervision of the pupils waiting lunch had to be provided but these occasions have been few. The problem might be greater if we were not an 11-16 school and had to deal with three-hour papers for 'A' level. Few 'O' level and CSE papers last more than 2½ hours. A pupil who happens to sit two papers in one day can, if the morning paper starts at 9.00 a.m., complete by 11.30 and thus have

1½ hours before starting again at 1.00 p.m., which is enough of a break.

Early in the experiment we had some trouble caused by our pupils collecting friends from other nearby schools but the novelty of this soon wore off, particularly as one local headmaster suggested that a transfer on a permanent basis could be arranged for pupils who wished to visit his school! We now leave earlier than the junior and infant schools on the same campus and some of our pupils wait for younger brothers and sisters from these schools. Previously pupils from the schools for younger pupils had been collected by parents or not at all – a clear case of a change in pattern creating a change in habits. Ideally, schools on the same campus should have similar departure times but, because of different organisational and supervision patterns which obtain in the junior and infant schools, they are reluctant to alter their school times.

The shortening in the overall time of occupation of the building during the school day has led to a significant fall in the consumption of fuel, an added bonus and a factor very pertinent to the present crisis both in finance and in fuel availability.

The school has a small catchment area and pupils do not make great use of buses, certainly not enough use for any special arrangements to have to be made. Schools which make great use of local bus services and of contract buses might find less difficulty in obtaining transport with the earlier leaving times. Schools which have a lot of pupils who attend from a distance do rely to a certain extent on extra-curricular activities taking place during the lunch hour. If the activities took place after school then arrangements for some of the public transport to leave later could be made, still lightening the load on the system at peak travelling times.

There may be other advantages and disadvantages revealed by a longer period of operating the changed lunch hour, but our own experience has been that if the organisational difficulties can be solved, then the problems created are fewer than the problems removed.

The Future

My ideal arrangement would allow that the dining room could accom-modate all the pupils who stayed to lunch, if necessary, for the whole of their lunch break. We shall start consultations on a further change which would do this and also reduce the need for single periods which, except for first-year pupils, are not popular with teachers and are time wasting. The change would be to have a day of ten 35-minute periods similar to the pattern shown below;

8.40-9.15	Registration, assembly, group tutor periods etc.
9.15-9.50	Lesson 1
9.50-10.25	Lesson 2
	BREAK
10.40-11.15	Lesson 3
11.15-11.50	Lesson 4
11.50-12.25	Lesson 5 or Dinner 1
12.25-1.00	Lesson 5 or 6 or Dinner 2
1.00-1.35	Lesson 6 or Dinner 3
1.35-2.10	Lesson 7
2.10-2.45	Lesson 8
2.45-2.50	Registration

Such an arrangement would probably have the 1st year and some of the 2nd year taking Dinner 2 with the 3rd, 4th and 5th years split between dinners 1 and 3. Timetabling problems might mean that 4th and 5th years would have to dine together but usually in this age group fewer stay for lunch in any case. There would be no need for a whole year group to eat at the same time although it would be preferable for the pupils to attend the same time lunch each day. With the co-operation of the schools meal service, the possibility of snack meals and wide choice might be made available to the senior pupils.

Arrangements such as those outlined may well be the suitable compromise to shorten the day with its element of fuel saving but still satisfy those who believe that the provision of a meal at school is a social amenity that should not be lost.

As a headmaster, problem behaviour in school is, for me, a practical problem, which is why I have concentrated on the 'nuts and bolts' of a major modification to our school system. Having worked this out in practice, I have been interested to find that other schools (and others involved in education) have been working or thinking along similar lines. There can be no simple approach to the problems one encounters in a complex institution like a school, but working at an organisational level means that one can, at least, get them down to manageable proportions.

9 CONFRONTATION SITUATIONS AND TEACHER-SUPPORT SYSTEMS

Robert Pik

Over the past few years there has been a noticeable shift away from the concept of 'the disruptive child' towards looking at 'the disrupted classroom'. Interactionist theories have dissuaded educationists from viewing deviance as an intrinsic personality feature of the child. Instead, these theories have encouraged a closer look at the context in which deviant acts occur, i.e. with whom and in what situations the child is proving difficult to manage. The word 'manage' is of key importance because, more and more, teaching is being viewed as a group-management skill.

In outlining management strategies to help teachers understand, cope with and, hopefully, prevent confrontation situations, I am aware of doubts in my own mind about the nature of the exercise. The teacher in me argues that there is a need for positive suggestions to enable teachers to control difficult behaviour in the classroom. The social scientist in me however, demands a more cautious and more questioning approach to the whole issue. What behaviours do teachers view as being awkward or obstructive? How frequently does the behaviour occur and with what intensity? In many ways my dilemma is summarised by Hargreaves (1975) and his colleagues who believe that although more practical help is needed, there is a gap between 'social scientists [who] are primarily interested in explanations, [and] teachers, student teachers and teacher trainers [who] are primarily interested in solutions'. However, in their efforts to warn teachers against dichotomising pupils into the 'well-adjusted' and the 'maladjusted', Hargreaves *et al.* have, I fear, ended up dichotomising teachers into 'good guys' and 'bad guys'. The former are called 'deviance-insulative' and the latter are referred to as 'deviance-provocative':

> The deviance-provocative teacher believes that the pupils he defines as deviant do not want to work in school and will do anything to avoid it. He thinks it is impossible to provide conditions under which they will work; if they are ever to work then the pupils must change. In disciplinary matters he sees his interaction with these pupils as a contest or battle—and one that he must win. He is unable to 'de-fuse'

difficult situations; he frequently issues ultimatums and becomes involved in confrontations. He considers these pupils to be 'anti-authority' and is confident that they are determined not to conform to the classroom rules.

The deviance-insulative teacher believes that these pupils, like all pupils, really want to work. If the pupils do not work, the conditions are assumed to be at fault. He believes that these conditions can be changed and that it is his responsibility to initiate that change. In disciplinary matters he has a clear set of classroom rules which are made explicit to the pupils . . . He makes an effort to avoid any kind of favouritism or preferential or differential treatment; he also avoids confrontation with pupils. He rarely makes negative evaluative comments on pupils who misbehave . . . He is highly optimistic, in contrast to the fatalism of the deviance-provocative teacher, and confidently assumes that pupils will behave well and cooperate with him . . . Whereas the deviance-provocative teacher dislikes the deviant pupils and considers himself unfortunate in having to teach them, the deviance-insulative teacher claims to like all children and considers it a privilege to work with any pupil (p. 260-1).

The only explanation we are given as to why some teachers wear white hats and others wear black hats is that the two groups have a 'different philosophy of life and a different philosophy of education'. Although Hargreaves and his colleagues criticise other social-scientific literature on the subject, it is not clear how this notion of two distinct types of teacher offers any more 'practical help' or reduces 'the teachers' sense of fatalism and powerlessness'.

Given that our education system might well need a good deal of re-thinking and restructuring, particularly at secondary school level, teachers still need some very concrete advice on handling difficult situations 'in the meantime'. Many teachers seem to be resigned to the fact that seeking practical help, especially from the so-called support services, e.g. Schools Psychological Services, Child Guidance Clinics and Social Services, seldom produces solutions which are either relevant or applicable to their own particular school situations. Each year these teachers dutifully attend in-service day conferences and lectures with such teasingly hopeful titles as 'Behaviour Problems in the Classroom', 'The Disruptive Child' or 'Maladjustment', only to leave these courses with what one could call 'the Chinese-meal syndrome', i.e. half an hour after the conference they are still hungry for workable coping strategies.

I have chosen to discuss confrontations because I believe them to be

one of the greatest sources of anxiety among secondary school teachers.
As a supply teacher wrote to the *Education Guardian*:

> One day I would like to find my supply teaching restricted to cover-
> ing for absences due to the common cold, or 'flu, and not as in most
> cases, to teachers escaping from the mental strain of trying to cope
> with impossible, unruly and even riotous mixed-ability classes.

By a confrontation situation, I mean the tense 'showdown' that occurs
when, in response to what the *teacher* considers to be a reasonable
request for a pupil to either do something or stop doing something, he
'digs in his heels', shows open defiance and communicates either
verbally or non-verbally 'I won't, you can't make me and I dare you to
try'.

The following are examples of confrontations drawn from suspension
letters sent to a local education authority:

> I asked Mark (aged 15) in a quiet and friendly manner to sit down
> and get to work. He continued to run around the classroom . . . I
> asked him, still very quietly, to leave the room . . . but all he did say
> was 'Piss off' and 'I'm not going'.

> Denise (aged 14) screwed up (her) paper and threw her book on the
> floor. I replaced the book back on her desk and re-opened the paper
> and told her that she would have to write on it. Denise screwed up
> the paper and threw the book on the floor again . . .

> Steven said he wouldn't go to detention (for an incomplete homework
> assignment). I said, 'Very well then, you will come with me to see Mr.
> B. (Deputy Head) right now!' He then sat down in his seat and replied,
> 'I'm fucking not going anywhere!'

Talking to teachers, it is apparent to me that confrontations such as
these have an intense and unforgettable quality which makes them
very difficult to dismiss at the end of the school day. Although the slow
learner in the classroom can be the source of endless frustration for the
teacher, most teachers are able to 'switch off' from the slow learner's
problems when the teaching sessions are over. The teacher feels that he
has given his professional best and will try again tomorrow. There is
seldom a feeling of apprehension about having to face the slow learner
and his class again. By contrast, a teacher who has had a confrontation

with a pupil usually experiences great anxiety about the prospect of having to face that child and his class the next day and possibly for the rest of the term. The incident may be replayed many times in the teacher's mind.

There are three related questions which are seldom discussed with teachers by the professionals who are meant to be offering support and advice either as part of the in-school support network or as members of support services available to schools, e.g. educational psychologists. The questions are: Why do confrontations provoke such strong, uncomfortable feelings in teachers? What precisely are these feelings? What measures do teachers usually take to reduce these feelings? By failing to tackle these questions with teachers, professionals have failed to understand or appreciate the pressures on teachers, or they have failed to communicate to teachers that they really understand and appreciate these pressures. It is therefore hardly surprising that many teachers are often unable or unwilling to implement the advice being offered — because the tone of the advice is unsympathetic, or because the actual content of the advice is judged to be irrelevant, ineffective or impractical.

Before going on to outline specific management strategies I should like to explore the three questions in turn.

Why do Confrontations Provoke Such Strong, Uncomfortable Feelings in Teachers?

I suggest that it is because in a confrontation there is more of the teacher *as a person* 'on the line', that is, exposed and vulnerable. The slow learner may sometimes cause the teacher to question his own expertise as a master purveyor of his subject; the openly defiant student challenges the teacher's authority *and* severely dents the image the adult has of himself as a reasonable and sensitive person. He puts a strong doubt in the teacher's mind about his ability to cope.

The following example illustrates this notion of the teacher as a person feeling devalued during a confrontation.

> This incident began around 11.45 a.m. Denise was provided with paper and a text for a writing exercise after a discussion period (in which she participated sensibly).
> (1) Denise screwed up her paper and threw her book on the floor.
> (2) I replaced the book back on the desk and reopened the paper

and told her she would have to write on it.

(3)   Denise screwed up the paper and threw the book on the floor again. I replaced it again and explained she was being asked to do something and should learn to do what she was told without getting angry about it. Denise's response to this was a chain of swear words ending in a clenched fist swung towards my face. But Denise's action at this point was clearly not intended to hurt me as she stopped her fist before it made contact with my face.

(4)   I walked away at this point in order to give my attention to the rest of the class. A book thrown by Denise hit my back, followed by several screwed balls of paper.

(5)   I picked up the book and returned it to Denise, taking the opportunity to explain to her that she could not behave in this way or do whatever she wanted to do when she felt like it. She replied that I couldn't make her do anything and I insisted that she had to learn to do what she was told to do. She threw the book at me again. I said that there was no point in being aggressive as it would not achieve anything. She swore at me again and I said I did not have conversations with people in that sort of language. I asked her whether she *wanted* me to hit her and I explained that I don't talk to people in that way. She replied that I wouldn't dare to hit her, and I replied that I didn't want to. I explained to the class that hitting someone did not achieve anything. Some of the rest of the class laughed, apparently seeing this as a sign that I was too scared to face up to Denise. I turned to Denise and asked her to come out in front of the rest of the class. She refused and said I would have to make her. I asked her again more firmly. I said I was not prepared to drag her. I continued to fix her in her eyes and she came out to the front. She faced me and before I could speak attempted to hit me in the face with her fist, and then went and sat down again. I went over to Denise and shouted at her that she could not treat people like that. I shouted that there was no reason to hit me since I liked her and did not want to hurt her.

(6)   At this point I resumed my efforts to start the class on their written work, before dealing with Denise. The class were all hushed in expectation at this point. Denise got up and proceeded to pick up all the paper on the rest of the class's desks

and then screwed them all up and threw them on the desk at the front of the class. I asked the class to read the first act of the play whilst I left the room (I was going to find a senior member of staff to remove her from the class). As I was walking out of the room, Denise followed me and shouted at me that I could not leave the class as I was supposed to be teaching them. I replied that as a teacher I was free to leave the room when I wished. She asked me where I was going and I replied that it was none of her business and told her to return to the room. She said I was going to tell on her and then hit me in the back as I continued to walk on. The bell for the end of the lesson rang as I was crossing the playground. Denise ran up to me and said ****. I turned to walk on and she hit me with some force in the back again. Mrs L. later dismissed the class, after discussing the incident with them (12.30).

Notice, in the above example, how the teacher tries first to secure Denise's co-operation by invoking the teacher-pupil framework of rules, e.g. I am the teacher and you are the pupil; you must do as I say. It seems, however, that Denise does not share the same basic understanding of teacher and pupil roles. She refuses to obey the teacher merely because she *is* the teacher. When attempts to control Denise by appealing to teacher-pupil roles fail, the teacher resorts to appeals on a person-to-person level, e.g. 'I don't talk to people in that way . . . I shouted at her that she could not treat people like that . . . Do you understand Denise, I like you and do not want to hurt you?' These statements are attempts to convey the message, 'I am a reasonable person and so are you. Let us try to work out our differences in a more sensible and less hurtful way'. Having these personal appeals rebuffed is very painful to one's self-esteem. Not only does the teacher now feel a failure because of her inability to shift Denise on either the professional or the personal level, she is also acutely aware of having somehow made a fool of herself in front of the class, e.g. 'Some of the rest of the class laughed, apparently seeing this as a sign that I was too scared to face up to Denise'.

The notion of how a 'class hushed in expectation' adds tremendous tension to a confrontation will be discussed under the second question.

What are the Feelings Experienced by Teachers During and After Confrontations?

There are likely to be three main feelings aroused: anger, fear and embarrassment. There is sometimes also a feeling of sadness after a confrontation.

Anger

The teacher may begin by experiencing annoyance because one pupil is taking his time and attention which he feels ought, at that moment, to be devoted to the other twenty-five children in the class. Annoyance quickly turns to anger when appeals for co-operation on either the professional or the personal level fail (as in the Denise example).

Fear

There is fear of aggression and fear of losing respect. The fear of aggression is often, I feel, mistakenly only viewed as the teacher being afraid of physical or verbal abuse by the student. It is important to recognise however, that teachers, like parents, are often afraid of their own aggressive impulses when disciplining children. Just as a parent worries that his child may have provoked him to the point where he might hit too hard or say something too hurtful and irretrievable, so too teachers are afraid of letting loose their full fury on even the most provocative pupil. Loss of temper is a double-edged sword: the teacher often fears loss of temper in himself more than in his pupils during a confrontation. This is because as a teacher one is meant to be the example-setting adult.

Teachers tend to speak about fear of losing control of the class more openly than they do about the fear of loss of self-control. There is fear of losing the individual pupil's respect and, more commonly, fear of losing 'the class's respect'. To a large extent, the degree of control that a teacher is able to exert over a class is dependent on the degree of respect accorded to him by the pupils. Today, it seems, teachers are more aware than their counterparts twenty years ago that respect from the pupils needs to be earned. Perhaps this is because many of the props which supported the idea of automatic obedience to the teacher have disappeared over the past two decades. Children are increasingly aware of themselves as people with power, rights and privileges who are entitled to respect. They resent being talked down to by adults in general and by teachers and parents in particular. Teachers, however, still fear being seen as 'weak'. Therefore, when discussing a confrontation, a teacher will usually say, 'If I let the child get away with it he will try it on again' or, more commonly, 'If the class see him getting away with it then others in the class will have a go next time'.

Embarrassment

Confrontations clearly produce embarrassment for the same reasons that they produce anger and fear. When professional and personal appeals for co-operation are rebuffed, the teacher worries that this may signify a personal weakness or failing. By definition, it is impossible for the teacher to fail privately, because an essential feature of the confrontation is the audience. (The notion of public failure is, of course, equally important in understanding the *pupil's* increasing stake in the confrontation and this will be discussed later on.)

A further and less widely recognised source of embarrassment is the teacher's apprehension that someone above him in the school's hierarchy might well need to be involved, either during or after the incident. Teachers often experience acute embarrassment when they have to call a colleague out of his classroom in order to help deal with a tricky situation. But even if no other teacher needs to be summoned at the time, and even if the pupil is not sent out of his class to go to another member of staff, the teacher may feel obliged to report a serious incident to his Head of Department or to a Senior Teacher later on. Actions taken during a confrontation which seemed reasonable and imperative to take at the time, are sometimes difficult to explain and to justify to colleagues *and to oneself* later on. Once the dust has settled, the events which triggered the incident may, in retrospect, seem petty, trivial or infinitely ignorable. In any case the need to involve another teacher is often construed as an admission of one's inability to cope with a class. I have found teachers in their probationary year of teaching most vulnerable to this pressure. Because probationers know that the senior staff are recording their progress, they are often unduly and unrealistically worried about having to ask for help with an unruly class. They fear that asking for help in this way will somehow go down as a black mark on their record. Further, if a probationer does call upon a senior member of staff to help handle a serious incident, e.g. a pupil flatly refusing to leave the classroom despite the teacher's insistence that he do so, the senior teacher sometimes appears to succeed so easily where the probationer has failed, that the younger teacher finds it difficult to imagine his senior colleague ever being nonplussed by a child. What is often not realised is that the confident veteran has probably, in the past, made every mistake in the book but has learned from experience which strategies are most likely to work in certain situations; he also has the 'formal status' of his position as Senior Tutor, Deputy Head, etc. To the probationer, however, it appears that it is only he who cannot cope.

However, it would be wrong to suggest that only young, inexperienced teachers feel embarrassment when asking a colleague for help. More often than not, a teacher with many years of teaching experience is assumed to be able to control a class. If this teacher encounters difficulty it may be embarrassing for him to admit the situation, and even more embarrassing for him to have to ask for help.

Sadness

Although less commonly experienced than anger, fear and embarrassment, many teachers have, in reflecting on confrontations, expressed feelings of sadness. There is feeling sorry for oneself, often tinged with bitterness, e.g. 'Why did I have to get landed with 3C for a double period on Friday afternoon?' Interestingly, however, a teacher may also feel sorry for the pupil after a confrontation. This usually occurs when the incident has led to the pupil being severely punished, perhaps more severely than the teacher had expected, e.g. suspension or expulsion. There is a feeling that if only he had handled the situation better, the outburst and its consequence might not have occurred. A teacher may also feel sorry for a pupil when he has some intimate knowledge of the child's home background. For example, when the teacher is aware that the child receives very harsh treatment at home, the teacher may well feel that he has in some way 'let down' the pupil by acting over-punitively, just like the child's parents.

What Measures do Teachers Usually Take to Reduce the Uncomfortable Feelings?

It is not the place here to discuss the range of possible disciplinary actions available to teachers. Rather, I want to consider how teachers deal with the personal feelings of anger, fear, embarrassment and possibly sadness which are evoked by confrontations.

The most dramatic effect of a confrontation on a teacher may be avoidance of the pupil and/or the class. Teachers may refuse to have a particular class or, more likely, insist that the pupil with whom the confrontation took place 'be excused' from that class. In taking this type of action the teacher must openly ask for help from the senior staff or the headteacher. A much more difficult situation arises when the teacher takes time off 'due to illness'. I have observed the vicious circle of stress leading to time off in many schools. What happens is that a teacher who has difficulty controlling a class (or classes) succumbs to the stress by taking days off school, ostensibly because of colds or 'flu. After several such absences, however, the other teachers begin to be slightly resentful about having to cover in their 'free' lessons. The antipathy which builds up towards the absent teacher usually makes it *less likely* that he will get the support needed to cope with the difficult situation on his return. This leads to greater strain and isolation necessitating more time off, and so on. It is important, therefore, for senior staff to be sensitive to this developing situation and to intervene quickly and positively with support for the teacher, and not leave him to struggle along on his own.

By far the most common reaction to a confrontation which helps the teacher reduce uncomfortable feelings is absolving oneself by attributing the child's disobedient behaviour to 'something wrong with the child' (usually 'inside his head') or blaming the child's parents (usually referred to as 'home background'). Many schools want those children frequently involved in confrontations referred to the psychologist or psychiatrist because they 'require treatment' to enable them to return to the classroom 'cured'. Teachers are often surprised to hear that a child whom they consider 'a thorough pest' in school may be quite well behaved at home. Although children and their families may value the out-of-school support and interest shown by a psychologist, it is difficult to see how this contact will lead to dramatic and enduring behaviour change in the classroom.

In the second half of this chapter I should like to go on to discuss various strategies for preventing and de-fusing those situations which can prove so traumatic for teachers and pupils alike. These strategies will involve the school as a system on three levels: the class-teacher, the in-school support network and the out-of-school support services.

Strategies Available to the Classteacher

From my own teaching experience and from discussions with teachers I believe that confrontations develop and progress in four, possibly overlapping, phases: a build-up, a trigger-event, a rapid escalation and a finale. The responsibility for the build-up or the trigger-event may lie with either the teacher or the pupil but both are responsible for the escalation. Consider the following account of a confrontation:

> [the headteacher writes] On December 12th, Arthur, together with two other boys, was very late for school. Mr H. saw him, sent him off to assembly and told him to report later. All three boys were given 300 words to write as an imposition.
>
> When Mr H. checked up on their record he found that Arthur and one other boy had not been late for a month and so he decided to excuse them because of their good record. When they reported he said he would excuse them from doing the writing since they had not been late for many weeks and asked them for the paper back. It then became clear that they had gone off without any intention of doing the imposition anyway because the paper was later found torn up in the school's Christmas card post box. Because of this attitude, Mr H. decided that the imposition should stand after all.
>
> Arthur refused to do this imposition. When he was told he would work in isolation to get it done in school, he refused. When he was brought before me and I told him that he would do it or be suspended, he still refused and I, therefore, have no alternative but to suspend him.

In this case the build-up is clear, i.e. coming late to school and having to report to the teacher after assembly. Although the teacher then decided to excuse Arthur from the imposition, it later became clear that Arthur had already excused himself from doing it. Was Arthur's tearing up the paper for the imposition the trigger-event? The teacher obviously thought it serious enough to warrant punishing him for his 'attitude'. On the other hand, might not one construe the teacher's action of retracting the exemption he had already given as the trigger-event? In any case, what follows is a fairly common pattern of escalating punishment and refusal to accept the punishment leading to more severe punishment, etc. The finale is the suspension. The headmaster states that he had 'no alternative' and I believe that Mr H. would also claim that he had no alternative to the action he took. This feeling of *'having no alternative'* is an important feature of confrontations. In the rapid escalation phase both teacher and pupil 'stake in' more and more, thus increasing the temperature, pressure and pace of the interaction. Note that at this stage in a confrontation, 'winning' and 'losing' become increasingly important to both participants while the notions of winning and losing become more narrowly defined by them. Things reach such a pitch that the teacher can only construe winning as getting the pupil to do precisely what he says at that moment – anything less is losing. The pupil, meanwhile, defines winning as refusing to 'knuckle under' to the teacher's demands; losing is giving in and obeying the teacher. In Arthur's case, even the headteacher gets drawn into a very narrow definition of winning which, in fact, is the same as Mr H.'s definition, i.e. making Arthur do his imposition is winning and no other alternative is even considered.

What rules about preventing and handling confrontations can we derive from Arthur's case? *Rule No. 1* must be: *decide first whether it is worth risking a confrontation over a particular incident. Has there been a breach of school rules or principles important enough to warrant intervention at that moment, or would a quiet word with the pupil later on perhaps be a better course to follow?* I am not advocating looking the other way when school rules are broken. I am advocating 'weighing up' the pros and cons of taking certain actions at certain times. In Arthur's case, the issue of lateness to school became a non-issue by the teacher's own admission. If the teacher felt that Arthur's attitude warranted punishment, why choose the same instrument of punishment, i.e. the imposition, which had already been judged by both teacher and pupil to be unfair?

Rule No. 2 is a paraphrase of Dr Benjamin Spock's well-known formula: *leave yourself and the pupil a gracious way out.* When there are no visible outlets or graceful exits available for either the teacher or the pupil, there is pressure on both to continue escalating the confrontation. The idea of saving face, already discussed with regard to teachers, is equally important with regard to children. There is always the danger of the pupil being pushed by the audience towards greater acts of bravado and defiance. The further the confrontation develops the harder it is for both pupil and teacher to back down. Often, therefore, the best move the teacher can make is to refuse to 'stake in' during the build-up stage or to refuse to increase his stake during the escalation phase. This may sometimes require the teacher taking the lead by admitting that he was wrong. It should have been clear to Mr H. that trying to force Arthur to do the imposition in isolation would be a further escalation. An alternative strategy, still available to Mr H. at that time, could have been to dismiss the event whilst still making his point. For instance, he might have said something to this effect: 'Arthur, you were wrong not to do the imposition I gave you but perhaps I was wrong in giving it to you in the first place. Make things easier for us both by keeping up your good record of punctuality.'

Here is another example of a confrontation:

At lunchtime today the Deputy Head reported serious trouble with a
teacher over misbehaviour in the House block.
   Clive was in the House area with three other boys who were from
another house and shouldn't have been there. They made raucous
comments in the hearing of a young teacher and then ran off. The
teacher followed and found these 13-year-old boys hiding like
children in lockers in a cloakroom alcove.
   He told them to get out and they sauntered off in the direction of
the exit. He followed them to see if they had gone out and hearing a
noise in the toilets, he looked inside to see that three of the lavatory
cabinets were occupied, but that Clive was waiting outside. When the
teacher entered, Clive went into another toilet cabinet, sat down on
the seat and made a coarse and obscene remark. The teacher told
him to get out once more and had to repeat this order at least three
times. Clive did not go and was quite obviously deliberately provok-
ing a situation.
   Finally the teacher had to warn him, 'If you will not go and I have
to take hold of you to get you out you will regret it'.
   Clive replied, 'Go on, mark me, I would love that'.
   Consequently the teacher had to take hold of Clive and with considerable difficulty began to lead him out of the building. By the
time other staff arrived, Clive was reduced to tears of rage and
frustration at not being allowed to have his own way. He continued
to be loud, abusive and obscene as he was escorted from the building.
When he finally left he threatened the teacher concerned with
violence, saying something to the effect, 'That is the way to get
your neck broken'.
   The other boys admit that they were all being provocative and
refer to the incident as 'aggro'.

I believe that the young male teacher involved in this incident was lured
into a confrontation. The toilets, cloakrooms and locker-rooms are
generally areas that adolescent pupils tend to consider their own 'ground',
or at least not the teacher's ground. The teacher is usually in a 'one-down'
position when trying to remove them from these areas. Note that it was
the teacher, and not Clive, who first made threatening remarks about
using physical force, i.e. 'If you will not go and I have to take hold of
you to get you out, you will regret it'. I believe that this teacher was
very fortunate not to have been assaulted by the pupil. (Referring back

to the Denise incident, the reader will recall that again it was the teacher who first suggested physical force, i.e. 'I asked her whether she *wanted me to hit her . . .*')

Rule No. 3 is therefore: *remember that threats by a teacher to use physical force or the actual use of physical force will nearly always escalate a conflict very quickly and dramatically and will greatly increase the probability of the pupil reacting violently.*

A situation which is especially important to avoid is a male teacher physically handling or restraining a female pupil. Consider the example of Mary:

> At the beginning of the fifth period on a Friday, Mr S. was standing at the door of Room J20 to control the movement of the pupils out and in when Mary, holding a plastic bag, tried to push past him in order to give the bag to a friend already in J20. Mary should have been in another room and was behaving characteristically in being where she ought not to be at that particular time. The (male) teacher restrained her, intending to call over the friend to collect the bag at the door. When restrained, Mary kicked out at the teacher, hit him twice in the face, tearing off his spectacles. The teacher made no attempt to retaliate, but Mary then pulled his hair and kicked out.

Even though the impression given is that the teacher's physical contact with Mary seemed quite spontaneous and not intended to be threatening, Mary over-reacted instantly. Physical handling, even something so slight as catching at the sleeve of a child's jacket may trigger a violent response.

Rule No. 4 is: *a reasonable time after a confrontation, the teacher involved should take the opportunity to talk privately with the pupil before they are next scheduled to come into contact with one another in the classroom.* There is obviously little point in trying to have a conversation while either the teacher or the pupil is still 'high' following a confrontation and so one must allow a reasonable 'cooling-off' period. In practice, what often happens is that the pupil is sent to a senior teacher who is left to deal with the situation without further involvement by the class teacher. Although this is a useful manoeuvre in that it allows for a cooling-off period for both teacher and child, it does little to reduce the teacher's apprehension about the next contact he will have with the child in the classroom. In a quiet moment, away from the audience, it is usually much easier for teacher and pupil to make the kind of contact in which they come over as 'themselves'. In this conversation there is little point getting hung up on the issues of who was right and who was wrong. It is better for the teacher to concede that both he and the pupil seem to get rather carried away sometimes. The message for the teacher to try to get across is: 'I regret that this happened; let us try not to force each other into a difficult position again.'

Some teachers may regard this as merely 'humouring' or 'placating' the child, when a 'firm stand' would be more correct. But desired behaviour is not brought about by confrontation: putting a child in a position he cannot move from is to confirm him in a deviant role. A child, like an adult, becomes what he does. Some children may need a good deal of humouring in this fashion but, at the very least, it enables them to keep out of a role that they would then feel they had to defend. A brief 'backstage' contact will greatly reduce the teacher's anxiety about the next contact he will have with the child when both will again be 'on stage'. The personal appeals made by the teacher and rejected by the child in the heat of the confrontation are more likely to be responded to by the child later on.

The reader will recall that in defining a confrontation I stated earlier that the pupil reacted with defiance to *what the teacher considered to be a reasonable demand*. Often, however, in the aftermath, the teacher's eyes may be opened to the fact that what he considered a reasonable demand was, in fact, very *unreasonable* from a child's point of view. One dramatic example of this was evident in an account a teacher related to me. The teacher had, in his own words, 'a real dust-up' with a thirteen year old boy.

In covering a class for an absent colleague, he asked the class to read aloud from their geography books. The second boy he called upon to read was still fumbling around in his desk for the correct book. The teacher waited patiently, not wanting to let the boy off the hook by calling on someone else to read. When the boy said that he did not have his book, the teacher went over to his desk and found it for him. Feeling that the boy was 'trying it on' and testing him out, and increasingly aware of the giggles and titters from the rest of the class, the teacher demanded that the boy stand up and read immediately. At this point the boy slammed his desk shut, sat back in his chair and folded his arms in a gesture of defiance. A rapid and intense escalation followed.

Ultimately the boy was sent to wait outside the headteacher's office. Two periods later the teacher chanced upon the boy still waiting to see the Head. He asked the boy to have a chat with him in the medical room adjacent to the office. He felt that both he and the lad appeared calmer to each other. From this conversation it became apparent to the teacher that the boy had refused to read because he was almost unable to read. The boy had managed to keep his illiteracy fairly secret to all but his closest friends.

Clearly, what seemed to the teacher to be a reasonable demand for the boy to read was totally *unreasonable* and embarrassing from the boy's point of view. The confrontation had provided an effective 'smokescreen' for the boy's problem.

Strategies Available to the In-school Support Network

Many schools have a specially designated pastoral-care team comprising Heads of Year, Senior Masters and Mistresses and/or Heads of Department. Very often these staff are paid an extra allowance for their pastoral-care duties. However, a school need not necessarily have a formal pastoral-care team as such; sometimes it can even be a disadvantage. The least-effective pastoral-care teams I have encountered are those that are construed by the staff as dealing exclusively with discipline problems, i.e. handing out punishment to 'troublemakers' sent to them by class teachers and form teachers. By contrast, the most effective senior staff, whether they are called a pastoral-care team or not, are those who make it clear to the staff that pastoral care is something worthwhile for all children and for all teachers. The role is one of support and guidance for pupils and staff. Matters to do with the curriculum, in-service training courses and academic standards in the school are seen to be just as much their concern as the issue of children's behaviour in the classroom. Teachers are seen to be receiving advice and back-up by the senior staff while being encouraged to take on greater responsibility for dealing with disruptive behaviour themselves rather than passing routine problems on.

   Senior staff have an important role to play in the management of confrontation situations. To begin with it is essential that all the teachers know who the senior staff are and how they may be contacted at short notice. Although this may sound almost absurdly elementary, I have found several schools which were so large and with such frequent staff turnover, that many of the newer teachers asked *me* – the visiting psychologist – for some kind of list or chart to clarify the staff structure of *their* school! No-one had ever told them who to turn to in the complicated school hierarchy if they required help in a difficult situation. Pupils sometimes received more formal induction into the school structure than did the teachers. Senior staff need to hold regular meetings and support groups for the probationer teachers and they should include in these groups teachers who are new to the school and its particular characteristics, even though they may have had a few years of previous teaching experience.

All staff, especially the probationers, should be encouraged to ask for help from the senior staff, sooner rather than later, if they are experiencing difficulties in controlling a class. Senior staff are in the best position to explain some of the points covered in this chapter with regard to the nature of confrontations and the feelings they evoke in teachers. Many teachers have told me that it would have helped them very much if they had heard from their senior colleagues that they too sometimes experienced difficulty in controlling a class. In fact, it took them some time to find out that they were not the only ones who sometimes found it difficult to cope with a class. This discovery, really more of a revelation to many of them, was acknowledged to be greatly reassuring.

As well as a support and advisory role, senior staff need to take an intervention role. That is, they should fulfil a 'call-out' function that classteachers can make use of if a confrontation escalates to a dangerous stage (I sometimes refer to 'calling out the cavalry'). Mark's case illustrates some useful points with regard to a teacher's summoning help during a confrontation.

When Mark came in, he immediately started to fight (not seriously) with Gary. I asked him many times, in a very quiet and friendly manner, to sit down and get to work. He continued to run around the classroom directing Kung Fu kicks at various people and jumping over the furniture. Eventually I asked him, still very quietly, to leave the room. He did leave, but returned very shortly and stood behind me. I again asked him to leave but he stopped listening to me and went and appropriated David's chair. I went over to him and tried to persuade him to leave, but all he did say was 'Piss off' and 'I'm not going'. He would not come out of the room with me and I decided not to touch him or use any force at all. I tried to phone a senior member of staff but could not contact anyone. I then went to ask Mr R. for assistance, and I had to stay to supervise his class.

Signed: Mr S. [probationer]

At approximately 14.00 hours today I was teaching 3C in D27 when Mr S. came in and said that Mark had entered his room, had hit some of the others and refused to leave. Mr S. asked me to intervene. I left him with my class and went to the class next door where Mark was sitting quietly in the far corner. I asked him to leave and his reply, as accurately as I can recall, was 'No, I'm not going to pick up any books.' This puzzled me and I said I didn't know anything of any books. I again asked him to leave and he refused. I said, 'Mark, I will ask you three times to leave'. This I did and each time he refused. I then took hold of the back of his chair to turn it (he was sitting with his back to me). He stood up and lashed backwards with his foot. By accident or design he struck the chair which hit my leg. He then turned and swung a punch at my body. This I parried and he backed up against the wall. We faced each other for several moments during which I asked him several times to leave. The Senior Master then arrived and took over.

Signed: Mr R. [2-year veteran]

The classteacher's initial handling of the situation seemed quite reasonable. He did, however, make one mistake in sending Mark out of the room without either sending him *to* someone or otherwise 'attaching' him. Just sending a child out in this manner usually invites him to stand outside the door making funny faces, much to the amusement of the class, and of course does not prevent his coming back in again to carry on the argument if he so desires. Unfortunately, in the present example, the system lets the teacher down badly, with disastrous consequences – 'I tried to phone a senior member of staff but could not contact anyone'. This should never happen. At worst, it should always be possible to contact a secretary and leave it to her to summon a senior staff member to a classroom as a matter of urgency. Or, a colleague in the next classroom could be asked to do this. Calling in a colleague who is not much more experienced than oneself (like Mr R.) will often only escalate the confrontation. There is a definite face-saving element for the pupil in being removed from the classroom by a senior member of staff and not by a junior member of staff. There is a feeling that 'anyone would go out if Mr B. ordered them to'.

A further mistake made by Mark's teacher, however, was sending his colleague next door to deal with the situation for him. If the two teachers had gone in together to deal with Mark at least they would have had strength of numbers. Instead, Mr R. is asked to deal with the difficult situation on his own and is easily confused when he sees Mark sitting quietly in the corner; he is even more puzzled by Mark's reference to 'picking up books', about which Mr R. clearly knows nothing. Why did Mr S. feel that he needed to cover Mr R,'s class during all this?

One other point worth noting is Mr R.'s tactical error in saying to Mark, 'I will ask you three times to leave'. Less experienced teachers often fall into this trap not realising that by stating that they will ask three times, they are begging the student to defy the first two requests! Only by waiting for the third request will the pupil get the confrontation back to the stage it was already at before the first two requests were made. Usually, teachers make three requests in order to stall for time. Like Mr Micawber there is the magical hope that 'something will turn up', e.g. a senior member of staff will suddenly materialise to help out – or the bell will ring for break. Senior staff need to be available to intervene in these situations. Furthermore, they should make it clear that they would prefer to be called out *immediately* rather than have to deal with a situation that has escalated into something more serious. Probationer teachers, in particular, will need reassurance that it is reasonable to ask for help in this way: that it is better to accept help than lose control.

Strategies Available to the Support Services

In terms of preventing and handling confrontations the educational psychologist may have a good deal to offer but only if he visits the school on a regular basis and is seen by the staff as being a useful adjunct to the in-school support network. Inviting the psychologist to attend occasional staff meetings or, more importantly, pastoral-care meetings, may often prove helpful. A psychologist who knows a school well, is familiar with its physical layout and its staff resources, is in a good position to suggest possible alternative management strategies for dealing with pupils frequently involved in confrontations. He can encourage staff to look for patterns in the confrontations; to explore such questions as:

– Does the pupil tend to have more confrontations with male or female staff?
– Are there more confrontations with junior staff and, if so, does the pupil's timetable show a large number of lessons with junior staff?

- Do there appear to be more confrontations during the more formal lessons or during the more 'free ranging' lessons such as art, P.E. and home economics, in which movement around the room, gym or kitchen is essential?
- Does the class size appear to be a significant factor?
- Is there a small group of his peers who might be providing a suitably provocative audience for the pupil in several of the classes during which confrontations take place?
- Is there a pattern of failure or difficulty with certain subjects which might be a contributing factor to confrontations during these lessons? (Often signified by the days of the week on which the pupil poses difficulties or is absent from school.)
- With which teacher(s) does the pupil get on particularly well in and out of the classroom? (This person, even if he or she doesn't actually teach the child could be useful in a counselling role.)

These kinds of questions may provide answers which will suggest possible management strategies. These may range from altering an individual pupil's timetable to co-ordinating a clear plan of action for teachers to take in the event of misbehaviour. In cases where the staff feel that counselling for a particular child may be beneficial, it is better for the psychologist not to take on the counselling himself; rather, he can offer supervision and support to a staff member with whom the child already has a good relationship if that teacher is willing to try counselling the child. The staff member need not necessarily be a member of the senior staff nor a trained counsellor. The important qualification is that he or she is the person with whom the child feels able to talk. If a teacher is willing to make this commitment, the psychologist must devote 15-20 minutes of his time on each visit to the school during which he can conduct a private supervision session with the teacher.

    It would be naïve to give the impression that schools are crying out for psychologists to work in this sort of way. Similarly, this form of intervention would not appeal to every psychologist. Some schools and psychologists still get bogged down with the idea of individual referral, assessment and treatment by the support services, and prefer a more 'traditional' approach; and clearly the psychologist must first establish his own credibility with the school staff. One way to do this is to organise in-school talks with the teachers, perhaps during the lunch hour, to cover topics *chosen by them*, e.g. social-skills training groups for teenagers. In this way he can make contact with all the staff, not just those senior members directly responsible for 'pastoral care' who usually liaise with outside agencies.

If this chapter has one main theme it is that of co-operation, mutual support and shared understanding in the management of behaviour problems in school. The educational psychologist is the most obvious, and the most usually available, outside agent for such a co-operative enterprise, but his role is not exclusive. An adviser, a social worker or a psychiatrist could fulfil a similar function. Shared responsibility is a characteristic of successful secondary schools: it doesn't eliminate all the problems but helps to keep them under control and, more importantly, reduces the stressful sense of isolation experienced by many teachers.

10 ANALYSING A SCHOOL SYSTEM: A PRACTICAL EXERCISE

Joan Figg & Andrew Ross

If ones uses the factory analogy, it is fair to say that there is no factory that functions in the same way as a secondary school (Rabinowitz 1977). In school the worker has to relate to anything up to six or seven bosses in any one day, moving the location of his work each time, and engage in different units of piece-work on each occasion. A school is a distinctive system in comparison with a factory or indeed any other large organisation in society. For this reason any attempt to employ systems-theory approaches characteristic of industrial psychology necessarily involves a process of adaptation. However, the authors feel that such an approach offers an alternative model for the educational psychologist working with secondary schools. The present chapter is an account of our attempts to put this into practice.

The project originally developed out of a sense of inadequacy that we felt as practising psychologists when we analysed our contact with comprehensive schools. We found that in trying to establish effective contact at the secondary level, all too easily we became embroiled in problems of communication, which reduced our effectiveness. This sense of dissatisfaction came at a time when we were also interested in looking at schools in institutional terms rather than just in terms of 'deviant' individuals. Our hope was that by relating to the school *as a whole* we should be able to initiate change based on the social psychology of the school, so providing a more effective and constructive model of working. We were also interested in combining all this with operating as a team and offering the school a chance to interact with a group of people from the School Psychological Service.

This was the basic premise we started from. Throughout the exercise we retained responsibility for our existing workloads and relied heavily on personal motivation and support from our colleagues to maintain momentum. The School Psychological Service team consisted of two psychologists and a psychiatric social worker. We felt that because of the range of demands on us professionally it would be better to make a formal 'contract' of our involvement with the project and, consequently, with the school. The contract involved ten half day sessions. Five of these were initially spent on a seminar basis looking at the available

148

material on systems theory and adapting this to our own use, as none of us at the beginning had the necessary theoretical background. The other five half-day sessions were spent at weekly intervals in the comprehensive school.

We based our project on the concept of a systems approach as described by Jenkins (1976), who breaks it down into four main sections: (a) systems analysis, (b) systems design, (c) implementation, and (d) operation. At the outset we had decided to run this explicitly as an 'experimental' project, where the school knew we were trying out the approach. In this way we felt we should be able to use the goodwill of the school concerned and so obtain a relatively conducive environment in which to explore this new model.

There is much expressed confusion about the psychological service as it now functions and what people perceive that it does (Topping 1978). Most educational psychologists would agree that we do not communicate clearly about this. We suggest that there is a need for a broader view and for the psychologist to see himself and his client in the context of a number of complex interacting systems. Most educational psychologists know their own 'system' and are dismayed when the service they deliver is not seen as useful, meaningful or appropriate. But in order to interact with the school-system and to find a solution to any problem, it is essential to know what is happening in a school at a level of detail. Jenkins points out that one of the main requirements of a systems analysis is the recognition and formulation of a problem. We decided that our nominated problem area would be the interface between the School Psychological Service and the school.

It was at this point that we approached the school that we proposed to involve in the study. We contacted the headteacher and discussed the basic theoretical details with him and the reason for the project. He was very interested but felt that if we were to proceed we should have to appeal to his whole staff. As staff meetings were not compulsory initial contact was made by letter and then we talked about the project at a subsequent staff meeting. We began with a brief introduction to the theory and then discussed what would be required of them. The response was good. Not only did the teachers agree to work with us but several agreed to give us extra time outside the five half-day sessions and to become part of the systems team. The systems team was an important feature and is considered in more detail later. After discussion with the staff, the basic contract took the following form:

(1)   Three members of the psychological service will be in school

one afternoon a week for five weeks.

(2) Members of the school staff will be asked to co-operate by filling in questionnaires, writing about their roles and describing how they see their communication channels within the school.

(3) The school staff will be asked to comment about their views on the psychological service as it now functions.

(4) The children will be asked to comment on what views they have of the school.

(5) A group of staff will be asked to give one additional hour after school to function as the systems team.

As was stressed earlier, the systems team was the centre around which the project then revolved. The team we envisaged consisted of (in the jargon of systems technology) a team leader, a user, a model builder, a designer, an economist and a systems engineer. We then translated the roles into educational terminology and the final group consisted of:

(a)	Team leader	(One)	psychologist
(b)	User	(Two)	class teachers
(c)	Model builder	(Two)	heads of department/year
(d)	Designer	(One)	deputy headteacher or senior mistress
(e)	Economist	(One)	headteacher
(f)	Systems engineer	(Two)	psychological service members.

In discussion with the people concerned it was decided that for this particular group the role of team leader and systems engineers should be taken by members of the School Psychological Service. With a different group it is quite possible that another pattern would be feasible. The input for the first systems-team meeting came from us but in subsequent group meetings responsibilities were shared and delegated. During this time we continually referred back to the stated problem, i.e. the interface between the Schools Psychological Service and the school.

In the absence of a standard 'end-product' or even an agreed 'model of good practice', we reasoned that a school's subsystems were most meaningfully seen as being concerned with support and authority and therefore aimed our investigations at the pastoral and administrative systems. No attempt was made to evaluate any of the activities in terms of educational theory since it was the pattern of interaction and the perceived activities that we hoped to uncover.

The task was broken down into five areas of study. First, we wanted to know how we were regarded and with what we were accredited. Then we wanted to know how the various posts of responsibility were defined by the staff. The next two areas were concerned with the communication systems between the staff themselves and that between pupils and staff. Finally we looked at the time spent by staff on a variety of administrative and pastoral activities. This breakdown enabled us to determine the 'formal' structure of authority within the school and compare it with the operative or 'actual' structure. The five areas of investigation are described and evaluated separately.

View of the School Psychological Service

The aim of this section was to determine the working knowledge and previous experiences of teaching staff with respect to educational psychologists and school psychological services. The reason for this was two-fold. First, we wanted to know where we were perceived within the superstructure of the local education authority. Secondly, as an adjunct to making sense of the school's pastoral system we felt it was necessary to know how far the School Psychological Service was regarded as a resource to this system.

In each of the other areas of investigation the views of as many people as were willing to participate had to be obtained. This necessarily involved written questionnaires which we hoped staff would complete after some thought, and without the pressure to adopt any particular response style. In contrast to this general method of working we were able, in this section, to be less clinical. We decided to use a structured interview and for ease of later analysis to tape record it. This method of recording avoided formality and allowed a natural flow.

Each of the three members of the School Psychological Service team were involved in these structured interviews which lasted between ten and forty minutes. The teachers we talked to were pre-selected by the school's timetable in that our visits were always on Thursday afternoons and we interviewed any member of staff who happened not to be teaching. In this way ten teachers were interviewed making up 30 per cent of the teaching staff. In all there were sixteen questions which ranged from asking about personal contact and benefit from the School Psychological Service and projecting school needs which might be met by the School Psychological Service in the future (see Fig. 10.1).

Figure 10.1: Structured Interview

1. Do you feel that contact with the Psychological Service has proved helpful or beneficial to you?
2. If you gained any help at all was this in the form of advice only, active intervention, or both?
3. Could you try and explain in some detail what particular skills you feel members of the Psychological Service have which are different from your teaching skills?
4. What kind of problem or type of child do you think that the Psychological Service spends most of its time with?
5. Do you see psychologists as people you can work with?
6. Do you think that psychological time given over to your school should be solely child-based?
7. Where do you think is the most suitable place for children to be seen?
8. As a member of a school community, what are your demands of the Psychological Service?
9. Are these met and, if not, where do they fall short?
10. As an individual what demands would you make of the Psychological Service?
11. To whom do you think the Psychological Service is responsible?
12. Do you think the Psychological Service has any statutory powers, and if so, what?
13. What resources do you think the Psychological Service can draw on when dealing with individual cases?
14. When a case has been referred by you to the Psychological Service, who is ultimately responsible?
15. Do you think that members of the Psychological Service are professionally trained? If so, what does this training entail?
16. Where do you think that the Psychological Service fits into the L.E.A.'s organisation?

It was not possible to classify or tabulate the replies to our questions as the responses were so diverse, but some general observations were possible. What was most apparent was the lack of previous contact with educational psychologists. None of the teachers we interviewed was a probationer and most had had several years' teaching experience, yet 7 of the 10 had no prior contact. The skills with which the educational psychologists were accredited were understandably rather nebulous. They ranged from the inevitable knowledge of specialised tests to a presumed special ability to communicate with people. Without exception the job of the psychologist was seen to be dealing with the problem child – the behaviourally difficult, the personality disordered, the developmentally deviant and the socially unacceptable. Specific learning problems and curriculum development were not mentioned at all. Some acknowledgement was given to the need for teaching staff to talk to psychologists in a supportive as well as problem-sharing way but several teachers regarded the School Psychological Service as solely child based.

When we asked about projected demands on the Schools Psychological Service the replies were uncertain. Basically the teachers were happy at the prospect that in 'exceptional' cases advice and treatment could be obtained. Since, in response to an earlier question, the teachers were unable to specify the psychologist's skills, it looked very much as though they wanted the School Psychological Service to be a repository for problems. This was presented in terms of helping, and typically pertained to children more often than adults.

The final few questions centred on educational psychologists' statutory powers, professional training, position in the local authority's organisation and responsibility for cases. Replies to these questions reflected the overall lack of prior contact but in general there was an awareness of the actual state of affairs. We were not at all surprised by the answers we received, but we did pick up more goodwill than we had anticipated. Given that we considered traditional school psychological service work in secondary schools to be at best limited and usually ineffectual, we had expected some hostility and negativism. The basis of goodwill indicated a potential for the development of the psychologist's role in terms that might be mutually meaningful and useful.

Role Definitions of Job Titles

In keeping with most other organisations, schools have a proliferation of job titles which convey function, status and responsibility. Unlike other organisations, it is not easy to appraise the global structure and place people within it. This is because the prime function of teachers is teaching, undertaken by all the staff. It is not possible to place them within the school structure simply on the basis of their major function. Similarly, almost all other functions are shared to a greater or lesser extent across all grades of teacher.

However, the job titles exist and people are remunerated differentially according to their *formal* position within the school structure. It seemed reasonable to ask teaching staff how they viewed each job and so we gave them a list of all the job titles we knew to exist within the school (see Fig. 10.2). Also included in the list were jobs of people who were employed by the local authority whose responsibilities were primarily to the local authority rather than the school as a separate entity. One

problem in dealing with educated people, like teachers, is their verbal
fluency and in this exercise we aimed to extract the minimum amount
of information necessary to define each job. To this end we circulated a
list of jobs with space for only a one or two-line reply.

Figure 10.2: Staff Questionnaire

Please tick the role(s) applicable to yourself *and* write a job description beside
each category in the space provided.

1.   Headteacher
2.   Deputy head
3.   Senior mistress
4.   Head of administration
5.   Upper/Lower School tutor
6.   Head of department
7.   Head of year
8.   Head of remedial department
9.   Class teacher (tutor)
10. Form teacher (curriculum)
11. Union representative
12. School secretary
13. School caretaker
14. School nurse
15. Parish priest
16. Educational welfare officer
17. Educational psychologist
18. School's adviser
19. Subject advisers
20. School governors
21. Staff representative to the governors
22. Housemaster (Head of House)

The idea behind giving you so little space is to elicit from you the most basic role
definition possible. However, please make use of the space below to expand,
clarify or to otherwise make comment.

Thirteen members of staff replied to this request and, in addition, we
obtained a copy of the official job descriptions for the senior posts in
the school. The result was at first sight disappointing, although significant,
in that there was a general lack of specificity when it came to describing
the majority of teaching posts. There was no difficulty in describing jobs
for whom there was only one holder (e.g. head of administration,

head of remedial department, caretaker, secretary, union representative, education welfare officer, etc.). The reason for this would seem to be that if a person is not sharing a responsibility with another he is better able to define his role and specify the limits of his function. The head-teacher and his two deputies were understandably unspecific in that they were responsible to some degree for every aspect of school. The heads of department were accredited with organising the curriculum and this responsibility was not shared by any other. The remaining group of teachers included form tutors, class teachers, heads of year, upper and lower-school tutors, and heads of house. These were accredited with responsibility for educational standards, monitoring individual pupil's progress, attendance and discipline. This group therefore had diverse responsibilities which were aimed at the pastoral welfare and academic progress of the individual and the preservation of the school as an intact organisation. These responsibilities were in some cases dis-charged through specific duties (e.g. marking registers), but for the most part this was not the case. A later section looks at the non-teaching time spent by staff in school activities and provides a complementary per-spective on job definition.

A hindsight criticism of the way we went about getting teachers' perceptions of their own and others' job is that we gave no guidance beyond the need to be brief. This allowed respondents to slip into a response set and so to define each job in the same kind of way. This was valid in that there is a huge overlap of function amongst teachers but it was not helpful in defining the differences. If we were to repeat the total exercise this section would need to be modified or perhaps removed. By way of modification, we feel it would be more useful to ask staff to define only their own job and to do this by providing a check-list of the core range of *functions* commonly undertaken in all schools. Such a list could include: specific teaching activities, timetable design and operation, curriculum development, examinations organisation, oversight of premises and equipment, ordering of supplies, representing the school to outside agencies, liaising directly with parents, checking on pupils' attendance, monitoring pupils' educational progress and keeping regular records, disciplining pupils as a delegated responsibility and dealing with pupils' problems other than those arising from the curriculum. Such a check-list could easily be accommodated into a matrix comparing job titles with actual responsibilities. Whether or not this approach would show up any significant differences in a more systematic way remains open to question. A further criticism of our method was that we failed to acknowledge the existence of graded posts which were not accompanied by a job title. In effect this meant that we ignored some Scale 2 teachers who were second-in-charge of a department or had other responsibilities such as producing a school magazine, overseeing a library or being an examinations' correspondent. As the school under study was small there was a significant overlap in that many holders of one office were also holders of another. In a larger school this situation would not pertain and care would be needed to include all staff with responsibility posts, as well as those formally holding office.

Staff Communication System

Following on from the perceived functions of teachers' jobs we felt it necessary to find out the channels of communication that existed and the key personnel within the system. Within a given organisation it is not necessarily the nominal holders of the key offices who wield the power, make the decisions and generally maintain equilibrium. One approach would have been to site ourselves within classrooms or play areas, wait until a teacher/pupil problem arose, and then record the ensuing events. Such an approach would have been adopted had the investigation been problem based. But, in keeping with what we hoped was a non-threatening approach, we decided on asking staff to whom they would refer given nine hypothetical situations. The questions are shown in Fig. 10.3. For ease of interpretation we adopted throughout the study a number code system which related to each post of office. Basically the nine questions split into three areas: personal support (questions 1, 2, 5, 9), pastoral responsibility for children (questions 3, 6, 8, 7), and child discipline (question 4).

Figure 10.3: Communications—Staff Questionnaire

1. If you need personal professional advice (e.g. legal matters, promotion, etc.) to whom are you most likely to go?
2. If you need currulum advice to whom do you go first?
3. If you are concerned about a particular child (non crisis) whom do you go to?
4. If you have an acute disciplinary problem with an individual pupil to whom do you refer this problem?
5. If you have a general management problem with one of your teaching groups to whom do you go to discuss or seek help?
6. When you are on duty and a disciplinary or pastoral problem arises which you cannot deal with at the time, to whom do you refer?

7. Who is the person who has most information about any specific child at any given time?

8. Who is the most appropriate person to talk to parents who come into school to discuss the overall progress of their child?

9. If you have a grievance about the way something has happened in school (organisation) to whom do you go if you feel it is not a matter to be brought up in a staff meeting?

The results of this questionnaire are quite clear in that 49 per cent of all the answers cited the top three staff (i.e. headteacher, deputy headteacher and senior mistress). With the exception of the group management and curriculum questions (12 and 5), which were referred to the heads of department, all other problems were referred either to the form tutor or to one of the top three. With regard to class-management problems 25 per cent of the staff abstained and another 20 per cent either did not know what to do or would tell nobody. Hence the support system was unclear to the extent that almost half the sample of staff felt unsupported in this key problem area. Grouping the questions as above, Table 10.1 shows the percentages and rank order of staff citations. Only the top three ranks have been entered because of the high proportion of variance accounted for. For a fuller analysis see Table 10.2.

Table 10.1: Teacher Citations in Answer to Questionnaire

	Support		Pastoral		Discipline	
Headteacher	50%	1	15%	3(equal)	—	
Deputy head	—		—		37%	1(boys)
Senior mistress	—		27%	1	25%	2(girls)
Upper/Lower Sch. tutors	—		15%	3(equal)	12%	3
Head of dept.	29%	2	—		—	
Head of year	7%	3	—		—	
Form tutor	—		24%	2	—	

It needs to be borne in mind that the response by staff to all three questionnaires in the study was only 50 per cent. We suspect that the same individuals replied each time but as the scripts were anonymous this point remains speculative. The fact that we gained information from only half the teaching staff does present some interpretive problems but the lack of clarity about support within the school for at least one-quarter of the total staff population is undeniable. We would argue that

Table 10.2: Frequencies of Citations

	Question number	1	2	3	4	5	6	7	8	9	Total
	Abstentions	2	0	1	0	4	2	2	2	2	15
	Nobody	2	1	1	0	2	0	0	0	0	6
	Don't know	0	2	1	0	1	3	1	1	0	9
1	Headteacher	7	3	1	1	1	2	3	3	10	31
2	Deputy head	0	1	0	9	0	5	0	1	1	17
3	Senior mistress	1	0	2	6	0	3	9	2	1	24
4	Head of administration	1	0	0	0	0	1	0	0	0	2
5	Upper/Lower School tutors	1	0	2	3	0	3	2	2	0	13
6	Head of department	0	6	0	1	6	0	0	0	1	14
7	Head of year	0	1	0	1	2	1	0	0	0	5
8	Head of remedial department	0	0	0	0	0	0	0	0	0	0
9	Form tutor	0	0	6	0	0	0	2	6	0	14
10	Class teacher	0	0	2	1	0	1	0	0	0	4
11	Union representative	2	0	0	0	0	0	0	0	0	2
12	School secretary										0
13	School caretaker										0
14	School nurse										0
15	Parish priest										0
16	Education welfare officer										0
17	Educational psychologist										0
18	School's adviser										0
19	Subject advisers	1	2	0	0	0	0	0	0	0	3
20	School governors	0	0	0	2	0	0	0	0	1	3
21	Staff rep. to School governors										0

the top and the bottom of the power structure are easier to locate and define than the intermediate positions. This may explain why staff resorted to the top three or the form tutors for support and help. On the other hand, there may not have been any delegation of power, with the possibility of real help coming only from those who knew the child best (form tutor) or from the top where executive decisions could be made. We did ask staff to say whether their choices of referrant were heavily, moderately, or minimally influenced by actual personalities rather than holders of office. Half of our sample indicated that their choices had been heavily influenced by their colleagues' personalities. In so doing the staff acknowledged an informal support system.

Although a 50 per cent response-rate was quite good when one considers that we were relying upon goodwill in a sensitive area, analysis of this section was limited by paucity of numbers. We should have liked to have been able to cluster and compare the responses from the various groups of teaching staff. We strongly suspect that support from colleagues is a highly complicated formal and informal system which varies according to a teacher's own professional standing. To ask a senior teacher and a probationer teacher to whom they would go for help with a class management problem cannot yield responses which are easily compared. The other aspect of such questioning is the threat component. Neither the senior teacher nor the probationer may admit to ever having classroom-management problems and, indeed, a number of our returned scripts took this stance. There is no way round the problem of denial, but we reasoned that we would get closest to the truth if we asked for anonymous written returns about hypothetical problems. Since different institutions vary considerably in their ethos, it is necessary to take advice on choice, and wording, of questions from the school representatives on the systems team. In this way the threat component is both acknowledged and minimised.

Pupils' Perceptions of Staff Function

We have viewed the teacher in the classroom as one consumer of the system in as much as his teaching task is facilitated or hindered by it. The other consumer, and arguably the only true consumer, is the *pupil.* In order to validate the patterns emerging from staff interactions and specification of function, it was necessary to obtain the pupils' appraisal. We had hoped to match the questions we gave to staff but this was not possible. Instead, we asked broadly similar questions which fell into the same categories as before (i.e. support, pastoral oversight, and discipline).

This section was completely taken over by the school staff on the systems team who organised the timetable to accommodate completion of the questionnaire by all the children in the school. The wording of the questionnaire was worked out at a systems-team meeting where the School Psychological Service members were reliant on school staff for the most generally understood and unambiguous wording for that school population. As a result we obtained a very high return-rate with minimal wastage of scripts. The children were asked to answer each question using a number code. In addition, we asked that all teachers be specifically named and this enabled us to expand the code to accommodate six 'teacher' categories for purposes of analysis. The actual questions are shown in Fig. 10.3. Questions 1 to 11 match the staff questionnaires, 12 and 13 relate specifically to curriculum and careers, and the remaining four questions probe home/school liaison.

Of all the answers to the first eleven questions 83 per cent of the variance was accounted for by four main reference groups:

(1) Parents or relatives   30%
(2) Headteacher, Deputy head or Senior mistress   26%
(3) Unspecified teacher   14%
(4) Nobody   13%

The 'unspecified' teacher citations comprised un-named teachers, and teachers who were named but who bore no special relationship to the pupil. We looked at the breakdown of citations with respect to the three areas of support, pastoral oversight, and discipline. The support questions were those which related to pupil-instigated requests for help. The pastoral oversight questions were processed twice; both with and without questions 5 and 9 which excluded parents and teachers respectively. Table 10.3 gives the percentage and rank order of citations. No distinction has been made between sex or year groupings.

Figure 10.4: Pupil Questionnaire

Answers:—   (1) a friend
                    (2) a parent or relative
                    (3) a teacher (give name)
                    (4) nobody
                    (5) a brother or sister

                                                                            Answers

1. Who would you complain to if you thought you were being picked on by a teacher?
2. Who sees that you do all your work properly?
3. Who do you go to in school if you are being bullied?
4. If you are having trouble at home who could you tell in school?
5. If you are having trouble in school, who might visit your home?

6. If you don't do your work who would you go to?

7. If you behave very badly around the school, who are you sent to?

8. If you behave very badly in class who are you sent to?

9. When children have serious problems who helps them apart from the teachers?

10. Who sees that you are behaving properly?

11. Whose job is it to make sure that you attend school?

3rd, 4th and 5th Years only

12. Who do you go to for subject choice and options?

13. Who do you go to for careers advice?

All children

(Tick the answer you think is correct)

Answers

14. Your parents will be sent for if you behave badly in class.

15. Your parents will be sent for if you are absent for no good reason.

16. Your parents will be sent for if you swear at a teacher.

17. Your parents will be sent for if you don't do your work.

Table 10.3: Percentage and Rank Order of Citations—Pupil Questionnaire

	Support 1, 3, 4, 6		Pastoral 2, 5, 9, 10, 11		Pastoral 2, 10, 11		Discipline 7, 8	
Headteacher, Deputy Head, Senior Mistress	25%	1	13%	3	8%	3	49%	1
Form tutor	2%	7	3%	7	4%	5	2%	8
Unspecified teacher	16%	3	17%	2	20%	2	14%	3
Head of department	1%	9	1%	9	2%	8	2%	6=
Head of year	1%	8	2%	8	3%	6	2%	6=
Parent	20%	2	47%	1	52%	1	16%	2
Friend	12%	5	3%	5	0%	9	0%	9

	Support 1, 3, 4, 6		Pastoral 2, 5, 9, 10, 11		Pastoral 2, 10, 11		Discipline 7, 8	
Sibling	7%	6	3%	6	3%	7	5%	5
Nobody	15%	4	10%	4	8%	4	9%	4
Contracted Groupings								
Friends, parents & sibs.	39%	2	53%	1	55%	1	21%	2
Teachers	46%	1	36%	2	37%	2	70%	1

Whilst the figures as a whole mask individual age and sex differences, the three major categories cited by pupils are the headteacher and his two deputies, the unspecified teacher, and parents. The unspecified teacher group probably represents the informal system whereby pupils relate to chosen teaching staff or are fortuitously disciplined by staff who do not delegate this duty. We found it surprising that the in-school and out-school barrier did not rigidly exist, with parents being cited for what we considered problems more appropriately dealt with by school staff. For instance, it would be difficult, if not impossible, for an individual parent to investigate and terminate the bullying of a child. Perhaps it was the lack of any clear system which resulted in pupils falling back on a predictable source of help, namely parents. Pupils, like their teachers, seemed to rely heavily upon the headteacher for support rather than any teacher designated with such responsibility (e.g. form tutor or head of year).

The four forced-choice questions relating to situations which might result in a child's parents being called into school did not yield un-equivocal results. Taking the five years as a whole, the pupils felt that their parents would be called in but the majority was marginal. We looked at the year groups separately and found discrepancies created by all groups apart from Year One. We presumed that Year One was so new to the school that they credited the school system with more power and singlemindedness than later year groups. The basic finding here was that Years Four and Five were sceptical of the school involving their parents for the reasons we gave them.

The amount of data yielded by the 17 questions, combined with knowledge of each pupil's year group, class and sex was potentially unmanageable. Even for the small school under study this amounted to seven and a-half thousand items of information. This raised the problem of data transcription and analysis which, because of the relatively small staff returns, we had not previously encountered. We eventually decided upon simple frequency counts and a display of the data so that it was open to further analysis if desired. Even with the present study's 400 scripts, it would have paid off using a format which allowed easy transcription for data processing by computer. The treatment given could then have been a straightforward factor analysis which would indicate the clustering of responses.

Staff Time Estimation of Non-teaching Activities

In the final section of this study we were anxious to find out if the responsibilities held by teaching staff were reflected in their daily activities in a way which could allow differentiation. The systems team prepared a list of activities and staff were asked to keep a record during a given week noting the time spent on each task. Over half the staff participated and we were able to separate the estimates into two groups: staff holding posts of responsibility and those who did not. The questionnaire is shown in Figure 10.5 and the results are given in Table 10.4.

Figure 10.5: Time Estimation of Non-teaching Activities

Please make a daily estimate of the total amount of time (in minutes) spent on the activities listed below:

	Mon	Tues	Weds	Thurs	Fri	Total
FORM PERIODS						
(a) Administration registers, absence notes, etc.						
(b) Welfare						
LESSON PREPARATION						
LESSON MARKING						
CLASSROOM ORGANISATION Displays, etc.						
SUPERVISION DUTIES Breaks, lunch, detention						
EXTRA-MURAL ACTIVITIES Trips, clubs, games *outside teaching hours*						
INFORMAL CONTACT WITH COLLEAGUES						
(a) General availability, sitting in staffroom, etc.						
(b) For specific purpose — pupil welfare, etc.						

	Mon	Tues	Weds	Thurs	Fri	Total
FORMAL CONTACT WITH COLLEAGUES General staff meetings Dept. meetings, etc.						
RELAXATION PERIODS						
OTHER ACTIVITIES (specify)						
TIME SPENT IN FILLING IN THIS DOCUMENT						

Status in school	Total number of timetabled periods taught Number of periods lost to cover absentees

Table 10.4: Staff Time Estimation

		'STAFF'	
	ACTIVITIES	WITH POSTS TIME (mins)	WITHOUT POSTS TIME (mins)
1.	All activities in school	2364	2382
2.	Teaching	945	1050
3.	Form period: administration	48	70
4.	Form period: welfare	37	39
5.	Lesson preparation	116	216
6.	Lesson marking	218	346
7.	Classroom organisation	60	64
8.	Supervision duties	96	85
9.	Extra mural activities	323	293
10.	Informal contact with colleagues: general	100	83
11.	Informal contact with colleagues: specific	48	17
12.	Formal contact with colleagues: meetings	91	24
13.	Relaxation periods	43	15
14.	Other activities	239	80
15.	All activities excluding teaching and extramural	1096	1039

In the light of the previous results in this study it came as no surprise to find little disparity between the groups. Time spent on specific tasks and the range of activities undertaken did not separate the groups.

However, those holding posts of responsibility spent less time in marking and preparing lessons — which they may have undertaken at home and not logged — and more time in both formal and informal meetings with colleagues. The reason behind the real lack of disparity lay, we felt, in the similar teaching commitment for the two groups. The average number of teaching periods was 27 for those holding posts of responsibility and 30 for the others. This was an average difference of 3 lessons per week or one hour forty-five minutes.

The implication for the future, as suggested earlier in the chapter, is to produce a checklist with a wider range of activities. Inevitably such a list must break down super-ordinate categories into sub-ordinate components in order to detect differences. We suggest that a time-based analysis is unlikely to be useful even under these circumstances as the amount of time available for administration or pastoral activity is proportionately so small. It must be the activities themselves and their frequencies which ultimately differentiate. The one activity which must differentiate is decision-taking and a more fruitful approach than ours may be to produce a checklist, not of activities, but of a range of decisions.

Summary

In contrast with normal working styles, our over-riding objective was to look at a secondary school as a total system without a casework bias. Since no existing framework to do this was available, we turned to industrial engineering systems theory which we modified on the basis of our own experience with schools. It was necessary to take an explicit aim and the one chosen was to examine the interface between the School Psychological Service and the school which, in effect, meant looking at pastoral and administrative subsystems from the viewpoint of staff and pupils. Because there are few parallel links between an industrial organisation and a school, we were obliged to pay close attention to the relevance of the borrowed methodology and, having carried out the project, we consider the following procedure to be fundamental:

(1)   Locate sympathetic members of one's own psychological service.

(2)   Form a small team and contract a formal commitment.

(3)   Obtain basic theoretical knowledge of systems theory and

explore its application potential.
(4)   Convene a school staff meeting and brief the teachers on objectives and the proposed method of working.
(5)   Make a contract with the school specifying who will do what and the time commitment involved on both sides.
(6)   Co-opt members of the school staff on to a systems team and devise a working brief.
(7)   Carry out the analysis of the school system as specified, and made possible, by the systems team.

In traditional terms the input from the psychological service may seem to be a large one: but the way of working is so different that it is not easy to find a basis for comparison. The involvement of just three psychological-service members was important in that we did not constitute a threat to the school staff yet we derived moral support from each other's presence. We were therefore able to put in maximum effort investigating their system without siphoning off energy to defend our own system. Despite the 'cost' of our involvement, we felt the returns were also very high. In the first place we gained acceptance of working other than as individual psychologists on individual casework, thus setting a precedent for future work in secondary schools. Secondly, the nature and quality of the information gained was only made possible through the methodology and, in particular, the coalition of psychologists and teachers in a team. The result of this was a unique insight into the school as a system with its strengths and weaknesses exposed. We would argue that because large institutions change only very slowly over time, correspondingly the information and insights remain valid over a long period; and so the psychologist working in the future on individual problems has an invaluable fund of knowledge on how the school system can be maximally exploited and where the boundaries exist.

In the way we approached this project the cost to the school was not high at the institutional level since the running of the school was not interrupted or modified to accommodate the investigation. On the other hand, personal costs for teachers ranged from participating in a fifteen minute interview to participating in regular team meetings outside school hours and undertaking much of the responsibility for data gathering. The benefits to the school can be viewed at different levels depending on how far the systems theory approach is applied. This project stopped at the systems-analysis stage which generated enough information about the school for an adequate self-appraisal of the pastoral system: the key people, the channels of communication, and the expectations of staff and pupils. We would argue that for the particular school under study the revelation that considerable job confusion surrounds various posts of responsibility and that many staff and pupils feel unsupported by the system originally designed to provide this support, generates enough concern to warrant re-defining or re-designing the pastoral system.

A systems analysis is the first stage of the organisational model. The information from such an analysis needs to be descriptive and capable of providing an evaluation of the effectiveness with which the system meets its objectives. The analysis stage provides the baseline data as well as illustrating any incongruities or aberrations in the system. It is then up to the management committee to decide whether the systems team continues with its next brief which is designing alternative systems (model-building) to fulfil the stated objectives. The most promising alternative system is then selected and resources made available to implement it. It is the systems team whose collective experience and responsibility ensures creative but practical innovations and the new system is monitored and evaluated by it in the same way as the original systems analysis.

The implication for a school is that the headteacher, when faced with the results of a systems analysis, then has the option of asking the systems team to design an alternative model and to follow through with its implementation and evaluation. In order to design a new model it is necessary to specify functions exactly: what the consequences will be in terms of what people will do. In the case of re-designing a pastoral system we suggest this means stating behavioural objectives for the activities of individual teaching staff and pupils, given specified circumstances.

Much system change is initiated with only the vaguest idea of intended outcome, and on the basis of untested assumptions about how the system already works. The consequences of such changes are usually disappointing and occasionally alarming. Systems analysis offers a more rational basis for action; for educational psychologists, we suggest, it also offers a more adequate way of tackling many of the problems they are asked to deal with at the secondary school level.

11 INSTITUTIONAL CHANGE OR INDIVIDUAL CHANGE? AN OVERVIEW

David Galloway

Theories which explain problem behaviour in terms of psychopathology in the child or his family have a deceptive simplicity. The same can be said for theories which find all their explanations in the school. Both are conceptually naïve. A central thesis of this chapter is that the distinction between an organisational approach and an individual approach is at least partly a spurious one. It explains, if it is not responsible for, many of the misconceptions about the role of teachers in creating or preventing 'deviant' behaviour in the secondary school.

Assessing an individual apart from his social context is not so much an impossible task as a meaningless one. Assessment of organisational weaknesses which fails to account for individual idiosyncrasies, whether of teachers or pupils, is equally pointless. Another way of looking at this is to consider two related skills that are necessary for successful teaching. One is that the teacher should be familiar with his topic, using materials and methods appropriate, in the words of the 1944 Education Act, to the pupils' ages and abilities and aptitudes. A second is that he should recognise in his teaching the relevance of differences in his pupils and in their backgrounds. The question is not whether to concentrate on the school-system or on individuals, since the two cannot sensibly be distinguished. The crucial question concerns the school's role as a complex social community in the development or prevention of behaviour which its teachers or society regard as deviant. The answer to this question will determine whether the primary intervention should be with the school, the individual, or both.

This chapter is an attempt to synthesise the most useful aspects of a systems approach with those of a child-centred approach focusing on individual differences. The first part deals with the background to recent developments, in particular the conceptual and empirical weaknesses of some of the work from which they are derived. The second part deals with planning intervention, and the third with the different levels at which it can take place.

Background to Recent Developments

The Limitation of Treatment

The poor prognosis for 'treatment' interventions has been reviewed in Chapters 1 and 6. But the effectiveness or otherwise of individual treatment, whether psychotherapeutic or of any other form, is not really the point. Two other arguments are much more cogent.

The first is that outcome following the 'talk therapies' is worst for pupils whose behaviour is overtly disruptive, the group categorised by psychiatrists as conduct disorders (Rutter 1965) and inelegantly as OVRACT by Stott (1975). This poor outcome is evident, from comparative reviews of 'anti-social' and 'neurotic' children by Levitt (1971) and Robins (1970).

The second argument concerns the number of pupils considered deviant by their teachers. In 1950 there were 582 places in special schools for maladjusted pupils in England and Wales. By 1976 the number had risen to 13,653 (DES 1977). The same period saw a massive expansion in the numbers of 'the veritable army' (Reynolds and Murgatroyd 1977) of helping professions, with additional facilities for difficult pupils outside the special school system (HMI 1978b). Yet there seems to be no evidence from research that teachers today are concerned about a higher proportion of children than before the Second World War (McFie 1934; Milner 1938). The increasing referral-rate reflects a variation on Parkinson's Law: the number of problem children referred to psychologists for special education has increased in direct proportion to the availability of resources. The Warnock Report also makes this point with reference to ESN(M) children: 'Some of the variations between [local education] authorities also suggest a relationship between the rate of ascertainment and the availability of special provision' (DES 1978).

Given that up to 25 per cent of children are likely to need some form of special education at some stage in their school careers, it makes rather obvious sense to work with teachers rather than to concentrate our efforts on a small and, as argued below, arbitrarily selected minority of pupils who are referred for specialist advice. This does not, however, imply any reduction of interest in individual differences. It implies that the primary objectives are (i) to help teachers recognise their own role in the events leading up to the behaviour they consider deviant – as described in Chapter 9 – so that (ii) they may adapt their curriculum, methods and attitudes to cater more successfully for the child or group of children concerned.

Within-school Studies

Recent research on the school's influence on attendance, behaviour and educational attainments was reviewed in Chapters 3 and 4. This work provides indirect empirical support for earlier sociological ideas about the development of problem behaviour. Werthman (1963) for example, has argued that discipline in schools depends on pupils and teachers accepting that the teacher's authority is legitimate *a priori*. Some pupils reject this premise, only accepting the teacher's authority if the teacher conforms to their own 'rules' of behaviour. Teachers whose authority is not accepted as legitimate regard the pupils concerned as deviant.

This theme was developed by Cicourel and Kitsuse (1968) who argued that the social and educational typing of pupils by teachers and school counsellors can launch a pupil on a school career of delinquency or failure. Lemert (1967) gave the term 'secondary deviance' to describe this process. Initial or primary deviance elicits a social reaction, or 'labelling', which in turn creates further problems for the individuals concerned, with the result that they identify with each other and create further problems for their teachers, thus enabling a vicious circle of labelling and deviance.

This process has been described in the English secondary school setting. Hargreaves (1967) has argued that two opposing sub-cultures within a secondary school resulted from the school's streaming system. The teachers at the school would presumably have argued the reverse case: that the existence of an anti-school sub-culture necessitated streaming for the benefit of the brighter, more co-operative children – but this view overlooked the fact that low-stream boys in the first two years were not on the whole united in their opposition to the school's value-system. Their opposition arose from the recognition that they had been 'written off' as examination prospects. Hargreaves commented laconically: 'if the examination is the carrot by which we entice the horse to run, we should not be surprised if the horse stands still when we take the carrot away'. More recently, Hargreaves *et al.* (1975) have described in greater detail the social interaction between pupils and teachers which results in certain children being labelled as difficult, and consequently forming themselves into a deviant, anti-social sub-culture.

One of the ultimate steps in the labelling process is, of course, referral to an educational psychologist. Gath *et al.* (1972, 1977) found that both juvenile-delinquency rates and referral rates to child guidance varied independently of the effect of neighbourhood. Galloway (1980a) reported massive and consistent differences between Sheffield secondary schools in the number of pupils excluded or suspended on disciplinary grounds. These differences did not coincide with differences in intake; policy and practice appeared to be largely idiosyncratic to each school. The implication of these studies is that the secondary school is the most important predictive variable in referral for specialist advice and in exclusion on disciplinary grounds – of greater importance than home-background or internal psychological factors.

This points to a central limitation both in the theoretical and in the empirical research on the school's influence on problem behaviour, namely that its scope can be as limited as that of the hard-line psychometrician. Traditionally, the psychometrician confined his observations to the child, with little more than a token nod acknowledging the nature of his experiences at school and their effect on his behaviour. Recent work has concentrated on the school as a social and educational system, with little more than a token glance at the effect which constitutional and family difficulties may have on the individual's behaviour and attitudes at school. Hence it can be argued that Hargreaves covers as limited a field as the educational psychologists he so freely criticises (Hargreaves 1978a). What is needed is a conceptual framework for assessment which integrates an understanding of individual differences with an understanding of the sociology and social psychology of the school.

Planning Systems Intervention

One Starting Point

Headteachers often admit in private that problem behaviour is exacerbated, if not created, by weaknesses or inadequacies in their staff or within the school's organisation. The trouble with this sort of admission, as with all other generalisations, is that it is non-specific. Teachers, more than most people, are concerned about immediate problems and are understandably sceptical about long-term goals which are only related indirectly to the immediate issue. However convinced he may be that the root of the matter lies within the system of his school, no head can ignore the immediate problem posed by the individual pupil who challenges the system.

Educational psychologists are in a somewhat analogous position. They too may be convinced that a school makes its own problems. They may even be able to demonstrate – to their own satisfaction if no-one else's – that one school produces deviants in greater numbers and of greater severity than another with a seemingly identical catchment area.

Educational psychologists have no statutory obligations. In theory their job is so ill defined and open ended that they can legitimately tackle almost any educational issue they choose and claim that it falls within their sphere of professional responsibility. In practice, their employers, acting on the advice of the DES (1975), make fairly extensive and explicit demands on their time. These demands almost all relate to the assessment and management of individual children. If the Warnock Report's recommendations are implemented, they will spend still more time seeing still more children. Educational psychologists may not like these demands, but they will not go away. Like headteachers, they cannot afford the luxury of ignoring the immediate problem of an individual pupil who challenges the system.

Yet acceptance of this argument should imply no lack of interest in the system. It implies only that the individual child is a realistic starting-point for systems innovation. An assessment of a child who has been labelled a problem can aim to answer three questions: (i) What can we do about Peter now? (ii) What can we do about Peter in the long term? (iii) What can we do to prevent this sort of problem from arising in the future? If one aspect of a conscientious headteacher's or educational psychologist's job is to identify the long-term and indirect implications of problem behaviour for a school's teaching processes and attitudes, another is to resist the group temptation to concentrate all their energy and resources on the short-term implications.

The argument can be taken a stage further. Galloway and Goodwin (1979) argue that slow-learning and 'maladjusted' children play an important role in the social ecology of the school. They identify weaknesses in the system which affect the quality of education offered to the more conformist or successful majority. An example will illustrate this point. An adolescent takes an overdose, and subsequently tells a psychologist that she is bored at school where none of the teachers are interested in her. Investigation reveals that she probably *is* bored at school – on entry she was placed in the lower-ability band, in spite of good attainments in several subject areas. Moreover, none of the teachers knows much about her.

Possible implications for the school are: (i) that a more effective review system is needed of the validity of the ability-banding system, with the possibility of more flexible movement between bands; (ii) that the school's existing welfare and guidance system is monopolised by pupils who present more overt problems, at the expense of children who are less disturbing, yet perhaps more disturbed; (iii) following on from the last point, that the welfare and guidance system has concentrated

responsibility, and power, in the hands of year tutors, who see themselves as problem-solvers rather than as leaders of a team of class tutors
and subject teachers (Galloway 1980b). As a result the system makes
no provision for every child to be known reasonably well by at least
one teacher, least of all a year tutor with over 300 children in his year.
Whether the girl's teachers could in fact have done anything to
recognise her unhappiness and help her find some other response than
an overdose is debatable. What is less open to question is the fact that
her suicidal gesture gives her teachers the impetus to identify the limitations in the school's pastoral-care facilities. Less questionable still is the
point that these limitations are likely to affect adversely many *other*
pupils, even though they will probably never draw attention to themselves in such a dramatic way.

One way of understanding problem events

It is argued elsewhere that the underlying principles in the assessment of
learning difficulties are similar to, if not identical with, the underlying
principles in the assessment of behaviour problems (Galloway 1977;
Galloway and Goodwin 1979). The argument is best illustrated by two
hypothetical examples, each of which might come from almost any
secondary school (though originally primary school practice was used
to make the point).

(1) Group tests of educational attainments and intelligence are still
widely used as a means of separating children into ability-based bands.
They are also used to identify supposedly under-achieving pupils who
require special attention. The limitations of psychometrics-based
assessment have been discussed elsewhere (Gillham 1978). Quite apart
from theoretical questions of validity and reliability, tests have a number
of practical limitations:

(i) Test content has at best only an indirect relationship to the
child's classroom activities; to take an obvious and superficial example,
success on a graded word-reading test is no guarantee that the child will
understand a passage containing the same words in a book. The so-called
diagnostic tests only partially overcome the problem. They can identify
weaknesses in the child's skills which require remediation, but not
weaknesses in the level and content of his day-to-day curriculum.

(ii) Following on from the last point, tests provide an inadequate
base from which to plan subsequent work with the child. They *may*
identify some children in need, though their usefulness in this respect
has been exaggerated, but they cannot identify *how* to meet the need.
At best they are one-sided. By ignoring the social and educational

context which is reflected in both the explicit and hidden curriculum of the school, they implicitly equate defect with handicap. A medical analogy is possibly useful here. A moderate hearing loss constitutes a defect. It can be prevented from becoming a handicap by appropriate medical and educational help. In the same way severe handwriting difficulties caused by poor co-ordination associated with 'soft' neurology is a defect. It may not become a handicap if the school's organisation and attitudes are sufficiently flexible to adapt to the pupil, for example by allowing use of a photocopying machine or, possibly, by teaching him to type. In other words, the environment has a major influence on whether a defect becomes a handicap. Recognising the limitation of traditional assessment techniques, a growing number of teachers are exploring alternative ways of understanding educational problems. In the primary school field these are seen in the development of 'criterion-referenced' observation schedules, based on the teacher's own systematic observations (Bryans and Wolfendale 1973; Lindsay 1980). The observations are of clearly defined activities, each of which directs attention to some specific aspect of each child's overall development. Unfortunately, the strengths of this approach are only gradually becoming appreciated in secondary schools. At this stage, though, it is worth noting that: (a) the emphasis is on the teacher's own observations, mostly derived from ordinary classroom activities; (b) the recording is systematic, and (c) the results can be used to plan future work with the child. It is also worth noting that these are three of the central principles in interaction analysis, and that the assessment is derived from the child's performance in his social and educational environment, and is consequently as likely to carry implications for that environment as for the child himself.

(2) As teachers become more aware of the limitations of commercially available reading tests, they are focusing as much attention on the suitability of their own materials and books as on the child's strengths and weaknesses. The primary question is not whether the child can cope with the book, but whether the book is suitable for the child. An increasingly popular procedure consists of 'readability' testing (Gilliland 1972). This has the advantage of alerting the teacher to possible weaknesses in his own methods and materials. These have been shown to be a critical aspect of classroom control (Kounin *et al.* 1966). Yet it also identifies children with exceptional difficulties, who may need more extensive investigation and help. If a readability test suggests that the comprehension level of a text is above that of most pupils, the teacher will modify his method of presentation (unless school finances allow him

to change the text altogether). If the pupils remain unable to grasp what he is trying to teach, he may go back over earlier ground to see whether their failure is related to inadequate learning, or teaching at an earlier stage. On the other hand, if they obviously understand the material yet still fail to make satisfactory progress, he may wonder whether the problem is one of attitude rather than readability.

Like the first example, this is an unexceptional example of teaching practice. Yet here too there is an analogy with the underlying principles of interaction analysis and behaviour modification. As with any well-planned and implemented behaviour-modification programme, the teacher follows a clearly defined programme which he modifies or alters in the light of experience. To put it slightly differently: '[we] are merely applying in the field of behaviour the same principles and skills which successful teachers have always applied less systematically, though not necessarily less effectively, in teaching more traditional educational skills' (Galloway and Goodwin 1979).

Naturally, the successful teacher is not only conscientious in selecting subject matter and methods appropriate to his pupils, but also aware of the subtle pattern of interactions which create the classroom climate. However well he knows his pupils as individuals, the principles of group teaching and management are equally important. This is supported by Finlayson's and Loughran's (1976) research showing that the poor relationships in high-delinquency schools tended to be between teachers and their classes, rather than between teachers and individuals.

The point made by Kounin *et al.* (1966) that the teacher's familiarity with his subject matter is critical to classroom control has already been mentioned. Equally important are two of their other observations. One is that variety in learning activities, techniques for handling the movement of pupils around the classroom and immediate recognition of what was happening at any one time ('teacher with-it-ness') seemed to produce good behaviour from both 'disturbed' and 'normal' pupils. The second is that the teaching styles which proved successful with the normal pupils also proved successful with the disturbed children. This not only identifies teaching style as a critical variable in the management of problem behaviour, but also disposes of the theory, popular with special school teachers, that a quite different approach is needed with 'problem' pupils than is needed with the more conforming majority.

Of more immediate importance, however, is the evidence that the principles of interaction analysis and behaviour modification provide a suitable conceptual framework for understanding problem behaviour. Regrettably, this approach has sometimes been associated with naïve enthusiasm and mindless application of almost randomly selected techniques (Berger 1979). It is always easy to criticise bad practice, yet bad practice should not be allowed to obscure the usefulness of the principles when applied appropriately. A fourteen-year-old boy in a mixed-ability class might illustrate how interaction analysis can illuminate the problems facing the teacher *and* the pupil. Observation-based assessment might reveal that his inattentive, 'clowning' behaviour is maintained partly by attracting a consistent negative reaction from the teacher, and partly by the approval of a few other disruptive pupils. Looking a bit more closely, we may find that the problem is most acute in maths lessons, the esoteric mysteries of which he, and the other pupils, have long since given up trying to comprehend. On the rare occasions when he does try to do some work, his teacher is either too busy to explain it in sufficient detail, or heaves a sigh of relief that he is not causing any disturbance and gives the more able pupils some much needed attention. Both the difficulty of the work and his teacher's strategies have implications for his future teaching and management, yet even closer observation may reveal that both are secondary to more elementary issues of curriculum and pupil-teacher interaction throughout the school. The maths curriculum for example, may be insufficiently flexible for use in a mixed ability class. Or the school's initial reactions to deviant behaviour may have created a pattern of 'secondary deviance' in which peer-approval has become more important than teacher-approval, and can only be maintained by further deviant behaviour.

Ullman and Krasner (1975) maintain that, at one time, clinical psychology was applied personality theory, progressed to applied learning theory, and is now becoming applied social psychology. The same may be said of the assessment and management of problem behaviour, whether in the secondary school or anywhere else. Coming from eminent behaviour therapists, the argument deserves to be taken seriously. The implication is that behaviour analysis provides a rationale on which to base intervention, whether that intervention be with the school as a social and educational institution or with the individual child. Unless derived from a careful, thorough understanding of the child *and* his environment, an individual behaviour-modification programme is largely a matter of chance, since it will have an inadequate theoretical background. The same applies to systems change. Unless based on a careful, thorough assessment of the weaknesses in the system, and the specific objectives for an intervention programme, the success of this too will be largely a matter of chance, and for the same reason.

The Support Team: Uses and Misconceptions

Assessment and planning require a co-operative effort, whether for an individual or for an organisation. The reason is mainly practical and applies whether the eventual programme is co-ordinated by a headteacher, year tutor or visiting educational psychologist. Information has to be collected from a variety of people, each of whom operates in a different social context. A disruptive, noisy, aggressive pupil to one teacher is a cheerful extrovert to another. Similarly, a full-time 'remedial' class can be disastrous if run by one teacher, yet highly successful when taught by another.

The psychologist's role is not so much to identify and assess the problem himself as to help teachers carry out the process for themselves. Specialist advice is occasionally necessary, but never sufficient on its own. A girl may, for example, have specific difficulty with aural discrimination. Her problem has obvious importance, which may be spelled out, for the remedial teacher's future work with her. Nevertheless, whether the information and advice are reflected in the classroom will depend largely on the relationship between the teacher and the doctor or psychologist who provides it. In acting as a catalyst, the outside 'expert' acknowledges that teachers know more about their school's strengths and weaknesses, and those of individual pupils, than he is ever likely to discover. His role is to give structure to that knowledge.

One thing that follows from this analysis is that co-operation in planning needs to go beyond a synthesis of ideas from teachers in different subject areas or from members of different professions. A pastoral-care system is likely to be most effective as an integral part of the school's educational activities, so that its primary concern is success and achievement *at* school, rather than problems *out* of school (Galloway 1980b). In the same way, support services from outside the school are likely to be most effective when they see the school's pupils and teachers as part of an interacting system that is not only influenced by the school's policies, but also influences them.

If this seems a somewhat banal statement of the obvious, it is as well to consider the role-differentiation envisaged in the Warnock Report (1978). Briefly, the report sees educational psychologists as specialists in the identification, and to a lesser extent management, of handicap, while LEA advisers are seen as the agents of curriculum development and organisational change. The extent of the muddled thinking behind this rigid, if not false, divide is seen elsewhere in the report, which advocates that educational psychologists should be involved in training teachers in observation skills. It is no more possible to distinguish observation from the curriculum that is being observed than to distinguish curriculum development from the success and failures of the teachers and pupils who implement it.

The point is not that the educational psychologist can do an adviser's work, nor vice versa. It is simply that both must keep at least part of their attention fixed on the strengths and weaknesses of the school as a social organisation, its policies and its teachers. In practice some advisers are more skilled than some psychologists in understanding individuals; some psychologists are more skilled than some advisers in the field of curriculum development. The important point is for each to recognise the limit to his competence – or perhaps just for the school's headteacher to recognise it!

Some Necessary Conditions for Change

Writing with particular reference to behaviour-modification workshops for teachers, Ward (1976) points out that teachers' co-operation will be greater if they feel that the workshop:

(i)   is *their* project;
(ii)   has the whole-hearted support of senior staff;
(iii)   is consistent with their ideology;
(iv)   does not threaten their autonomy, for instance by excessive critical feed-back;
(v)   is likely to reduce their burdens;
(vi)   gives them a chance to contribute at the planning stage;
(vii)   involves professional trust and confidence;
(viii) is conducted in an open-minded way so as to allow revision as necessary.

These conditions are not specific to workshops in behaviour modification. They apply equally to workshops in any other topic, and to any programme of intervention which threatens the *status quo*. Almost by definition, change creates problems of re-adjustment, with associated stress. When problem behaviour has already threatened the teachers' personal autonomy and confidence, organisational or attitudinal change is likely to be doubly threatening. It is likely to flourish only when staff have sufficient confidence in themselves and in their colleagues to give and accept criticism in a mutually supportive atmosphere. Unfortunately, if the last statement is valid, intervention has least chance of success in schools where it is most needed. To some extent this is probably true. There may well be some schools in which intervention will not extend beyond the level of the individual teacher and his classroom.

One further point arises here. This is that systems intervention is at least as demanding in terms of background skills in forming relationships with clients as individualised approaches to treatment. An interesting research topic would be to see whether the educational psychologists who were most successful in the field of systems intervention were also the most successful at individual treatment.

Levels of Intervention

The Endless Quest for Bigger and Better Hawthorne Effects

One of the few consistent themes to emerge from research on the teaching of reading is that innovation, high motivation and progress are closely and positively correlated. Evaluation of the Initial Teaching Alphabet, for example, was very largely a problem of distinguishing the effect of the system itself from that of the evangelical fervour of some of its early advocates. Though less well documented, the same can be said of many of the innovations in the management of problem behaviour since the 1944 Education Act discovered 'maladjustment' (or, at least, gave it a respectable name). Chapter 7, for example, has described the limitations of withdrawal units for disruptive pupils while also drawing attention to their more constructive uses. As in every other response to problem behaviour, there is a danger that the sense of achievement in *doing something* becomes an end in itself, independent of any results that may, or may not, be achieved from the innovation.

In view of the lack of serious evaluation studies in the field of problem behaviour, it is perhaps over-generous to refer to the Hawthorne effect. That study, after all, demonstrated change in the desired direction. The lack of serious evaluation nevertheless strengthens the argument for a clear conceptual framework when planning intervention. As Rabinowitz has pointed out in Chapter 5, withdrawal units can be useful when established with specific objectives in response to specific needs. If, however, they are established as an administrative response to problem behaviour, they are unlikely to be any more demonstrably beneficial than other administrative responses, such as new schools for maladjusted children or increased numbers of educational psychologists or social workers.

Change at Classroom Level

Perhaps few people would see a classroom behaviour-modification programme aimed at a single child as an example of systems change. A more common response might be to criticise it for being excessively child-orientated, failing to tackle problems in the system (Quicke 1976). A cursory glance through the literature will show this to be a misconception. Even in the earliest reported programmes the primary focus was on the *teacher's* behaviour. Change in the child's behaviour was secondary to this. The programme described by Zimmerman and Zimmerman (1962), for example, succeeded because the teacher was taught how to alter her interaction with a child whose bizarre spelling was maintained by her attention. One can wrap it up in all kinds of scientific jargon, but the effect of the programme was to help the teacher become a more successful teacher. One of the most constructive uses of interaction analysis in schools lies in its scope for identifying the variables which mediate successful – as well as unsuccessful – practice.

Evidence from interaction analysis may well incriminate aspects of the school's policy or the attitudes of individual teachers. Nevertheless the starting point for intervention is determined by *what is possible in practice* rather than by *what is desirable in theory*. Two questions are particularly important. The first has already been hinted at, and concerns the motivation of the teachers concerned. Change creates stress, particularly when imposed from above by a headteacher or introduced from outside by a visiting educational psychologist. The idea of changing particular aspects of teaching method in order to cope more successfully with a few difficult pupils is often less threatening than the idea of re-thinking basic policies and attitudes.

The second question concerns the experience of the teacher or psychologist responsible for intervention. Implementing behavioural change at classroom level is facilitated by a readily available technology which does not exist in as well developed a form at institutional level. The technology must not be confused with the – often forgotten – underlying principles which determine its appropriate application. Nevertheless, its existence makes the classroom a suitable starting-point for systems change. It pays to make haste slowly.

Change in Processes

Change at the classroom level, discussed above, generally occurs through the mediation of a senior teacher such as year tutor or deputy head. A child is referred as a problem, and subsequent discussion identifies the situations in which, and people with whom, the difficulties occur. Insofar as the individual class tutor or subject teacher is the basic unit of pastoral care, this is not only inevitable but also desirable. Teachers at 'middle management' level, i.e. heads of departments and teachers with special responsibility for pastoral care, wield greater influence within a secondary school, yet are close enough to the shop floor to know, and influence, what really happens. This may not always be quite the same as the school's senior management would like to believe. If the process of pastoral care is to change, and with it the overall climate which influences the development of problems in the first place, the co-operation of this middle group is essential.

Even more than educational psychologists, year tutors or other teachers with special responsibility for guidance and welfare, can find themselves running round in ever decreasing circles trying to solve insoluble problems. This becomes almost inevitable when their role is defined in terms of responsibility for investigating and dealing with problem behaviour. Chapter 9 has pointed out the dangers of accepting the role of 'hatchet-men' – one school included 'punishment of offenders' in the job description – or as untrained social workers or psychologists. As Reynolds and Murgatroyd (1977) have suggested, their activities may be counter-productive by reducing the responsibility, and hence commitment, of other teachers to deal with problems themselves. A more constructive model for the year tutor is as leader, or co-ordinator of a team of class tutors, where the primary emphasis is on achievement and success at school, and only on psycho-social problems in the pupils or their families insofar as they militate against the primary emphasis. Defining the year tutor's priorities in this way breaks down the artificial division between 'academic' and 'pastoral' responsibility which confuses relationships in some schools. It also enables him to direct part of his energy towards other tension-creating aspects of school organisation, as described in Chapters 5 and 8.

Change in Organisational Structure

Evidence from recent research suggests that a school's *formal* organisation has little influence on pupils' behaviour or attainments. Neither policy on ability banding, for example, nor the outward structure of the pastoral-care system were associated with the varying achievements of twelve ILEA schools (Rutter *et al.* 1979). As Janet Ouston points out in Chapter 4, the critical variables appeared to lie in the school's ethos, or 'hidden curriculum'. Thus, curriculum content appeared to be less important than the manner in which lessons were taught, for example whether they started punctually, and whether achievement was possible, expected, and outwardly acknowledged. Similarly, the tidyness and general décor in the buildings appeared more important than their age or size.

The results of the *Fifteen Thousand Hours* study are consistent, except in fairly minor details, with those reported by Reynolds and Sullivan. They seem to imply that the key areas for systems change correspond to those discussed in the last two sections – the classroom, and aspects of day-to-day social organisation which help to create the school's climate. We cannot look to research to justify change in the school's *formal* organisational structure. The reason is obvious enough. The success of a system, whether it consists of a maths curriculum or a pastoral-care structure, depends less on the framework itself than on the attitudes, enthusiasm and commitment of the people operating within it.

The development of an anti-school sub-culture, graphically described by Hargreaves (1967), was quite possibly due not to the school's streaming policy *per se*, but to the fact that the lower-stream pupils recognised that their teachers regarded them as second-class citizens. The proper focus of systems intervention in such a case might be on the *attitudes* rather than on the *organisational structure*. This is not to deny that some structures may facilitate the development of problem behaviour while others have an inhibiting effect. (I happen to share Hargreaves's belief that streaming facilitates anti-social attitudes in less able pupils.) The facts nevertheless remain:

(i)   that change in organisational structure offers no guarantee of reduction in problem behaviour;

(ii)   that such change can only take place with the headteacher's active support and a modicum of cautious acquiescence from his colleagues;

(iii) that far-reaching developments are possible without touching the school's basic organisational structure.

Summary and Conclusions

A central argument throughout this chapter has been that efforts to tackle problem behaviour at an individual level are not inconsistent with attempts to tackle it by modifying the social or educational context in which it occurs. Indeed it is possible to go further still, arguing that attempts to change an individual pupil are likely to be successful only if it is first possible to change the attitudes and behaviour of his teachers. The question is not whether to adopt an organisational approach or an individualised one, as two incompatible alternatives. The question is rather one of priorities, in which the eventual decision results from an assessment of the interaction between constitutional variables, family variables and the complex network of relationships and expectations that create school climate. It is suggested that interaction provides a suitable conceptual framework for such an assessment.

The level at which intervention takes place is, however, also influenced by relationships between staff and by their general levels of confidence and morale. Initially it may be desirable to focus attention at classroom level, even though previous assessment has suggested that problem behaviour in the classroom is heavily influenced by attitudinal and organisational factors outside it. Creating a school climate which inhibits problem behaviour depends less on the form of organisation than on the way it is implemented. It follows that systems intervention, like individual treatment, has a better prognosis if its goals are specific, limited, and directed at detail, provided there is a comprehensive view of the changes that are being pursued.

REFERENCES

Acton, T.A. (1980) 'Educational Criteria of Success.' *Educational Research, 22*, 163-9

APTS Newsletter (1979) 'Croydon – Signpost to a Better Future.' *APTS Newsletter, 1*, 6.

Ashby, W.R. (1956) *An Introduction to Cybernetics.* New York: John Wiley.

Averch, H. *et al.* (1971) *How Effective is Schooling?* Santa Monica: Rand Corporation.

Baldwin, J. (1972) 'Delinquent Schools in Tower Hamlets: a Critique.' *British Journal of Criminology, 12*, 399-401.

Benn, C. and Simon, B. (1970) *Half Way There.* Harmondsworth: Penguin Books.

Berger, M. (1976) 'Teacher Education and Classroom Difficulties.' Unpublished paper.

Berger, M. (1979) 'Behaviour Modification in Education and Professional Practice: the Dangers of a Mindless Technology.' *Bulletin of the British Psychological Society, 32*, 418-24.

Berger, M., Yule, W. and Wigley, V. (1977) *The Teacher-Child Interaction Project.* Report to the Inner London Education Authority.

Bernbaum, G. (1979) *Knowledge and Ideology in the Sociology of Education.* London: Macmillan.

Bernstein, B. (1970) 'Education Cannot Compensate for Society.' *New Society, 387*, 344-7.

Born, R. and Sawyer, C. (1979) 'Time Contracting: a Method for Controlling Referral from Schools.' *Journal of the Association of Educational Psychologists, 5*, 1, 17-21.

Bowles, S. and Gintis, H. (1976) *Schooling in Capitalist America.* London: Routledge & Kegan Paul.

Boxall, M. (1976) *The Nurture Group in the Primary School.* London: ILEA.

Brookover, W.B. and Lezotte, L.W. (1976) *Changes in School Characteristics Coincident with Changes in Student Achievement.* Michigan: College of Urban Development, Michigan State University.

Bruce, N. (1978) 'The Scottish Children's Panels and Their Critics.' *Journal of Adolescence, 1*, 243-58.

Bryans, T. and Wolfendale, S. (1973) *Guide-lines for Teachers.* Croydon: Reading and Language Development Centre.

Buckley, W. (1967) *Sociology and Modern Systems Theory.* Englewood Cliffs: Prentice-Hall.

Burden, R.L. (1978) 'Schools' Systems Analysis: a Project-centred Approach' in B. Gillham (ed.) *Reconstructing Educational Psychology.* London: Croom Helm.

Burden, R.L. (1979a) 'How to Carry Out a School-based Systems Analysis.' Internal document. Exeter: University of Exeter School of Education.

Burden, R.L. (1979b) 'The Educational Psychologist as a Systems Analyst: the Totnes Project.' Paper presented at the Annual Priorsfield Fellowship Conference, University of Birmingham.

Burstall, C. (1970) 'French in the Primary School: Some Early Findings.' *Journal of Curriculum Studies, 2*, 48-58.

Byrne, D.S. and Williamson, W. (1975) *The Poverty of Education.* London: Martin Robertson.

Carkhuff, R.R. and Berenson, B.G. (1967) *Beyond Counselling and Therapy.* New York: Holt, Rinehart & Winston.

Central Advisory Council for Education (1963) *Half our Future* (The Newsom Report). London: HMSO.

Central Advisory Council for Education (1967) *Children and their Primary Schools* (The Plowden Report). London: HMSO.

Cicourel, H.V. and Kitsuse, J.I. (1968) 'The Social Organisation of the High School and Deviant Adolescent Careers' in E. Rubington and M. Weinberg (eds) *Deviance: The Interactionist Perspective.* New York: Macmillan.

Clarke, A. (ed.) (1980) 'Social Democratic Delinquents and Fabian Families in National Deviancy Conference' in *Permissiveness and Control.* London: Macmillan.

Clegg, A. and Megson, B. (1968) *Children in Distress.* Harmondsworth: Penguin Books.

Cloward, R. and Ohlin, L.A. (1961) *Delinquency and Opportunity.* London: Routledge & Kegan Paul.

Cohen, A. (1955) *Delinquent Boys.* Chicago: Free Press.

Cohen, A.K. (1965) 'The Sociology of the Deviant Act: Anomie Theory and Beyond.' *American Sociological Review, 30,* 9-12.

Coleman, J.S. *et al.* (1966) *Equality of Educational Opportunity.* Washington: US Government Printing Office.

Coleman, J.S. (1975) 'Methods and results in the I.E.A. studies.' *Review of Educational Research, 45,* 335-86.

Committee on Higher Education (1963) *Higher Education* (Robbins Report). London: HMSO.

Cornish, D.B. and Clarke, R.V.G. (1975) *Residential Treatment and its Effects on Delinquency.* London: HMSO.

Cox, T. (1977) 'The nature and management of stress in schools', in *The Management of Stress in Schools.* Education Department Conference Report, Clywd County Council, Mold.

Crosland, A. (1974) *Socialism Now.* London: Jonathan Cape.

Dale, R. (1972) *The Culture of the School.* Open University Educational Studies Course E282 'School and Society'.

Davie, R. *et al.* (1972) *From Birth to Seven.* London: Longman.

Department of Education and Science (1972) *Report of the Central Advisory Council for Education.* London: HMSO.

Department of Education and Science (1972) *Education for Expansion.* London: HMSO.

Department of Education and Science (1975) 'The Discovery of Children Requiring Special Education.' *Circular 2/75.* London: DES.

Department of Education and Science (1977) *Statistics of Education 1976 Vol. 1: Schools.* London: HMSO.

Department of Education and Science (1978) *Special Educational Needs* (The Warnock Report). London: HMSO.

Department of Health and Social Security (1979) *Children in Care in England and Wales, March 1978.* London: HMSO.

Division of Educational and Child Psychology (1977) Account of discussion of Hargreaves' paper 'The Deviant Pupil in the Secondary School'. *Occasional Papers of the Division of Educational and Child Psychology of the British Psychological Society, 12,* 554-7.

Douglas, J.W.B. (1968) *All Our Future.* London: Peter Davies.

Dyer, H.S. (1968) 'School Factors and Equal Educational Opportunity.' *Harvard Educational Review, 38,* 38-56.

Eggleston, J. (1977) *The Ecology of the School.* London: Methuen.

Essen, J., Fogelman, K. and Head, J. (1978) 'Childhood Housing Experiences and

School Attainment.' *Child Care, Health and Development, 4*, 41-58.

Evans, M., Wilson, M., Dawson, R.L. and Kiek, J.S. (1978) 'Schools Council Project: The Education of Disturbed Pupils in England and Wales: The Work of Special Classes and Units.' *Journal of the Association of Workers with Maladjusted Children, 6*, 1.

Eysenck, H.J. (1952) 'The Effects of Psychotherapy: an Evaluation.' *Journal of Consulting Psychology, 16*, 319-24.

Eysenck, H.J. (1964) *Crime and Personality*. London: Routledge & Kegan Paul.

Eysenck, H.J. and Eysenck, S.B.G. (1975) *Manual of the Eysenck Personality Questionnaire*. London: Hodder & Stoughton.

Farrington, D. (1973) 'Delinquency Begins at Home.' *New Society, 21*, 495-7.

Fawcett, R. (1979) 'The Educational Psychologist and Child Guidance.' *Journal of the Association of Educational Psychologists, 5*, 1, 8-12.

Ferge, S. (1977) 'School Systems and School Reforms', in A. Kloskowska (ed.) *Education in a Changing Society*. London: Sage.

Finlayson, D.S. and Loughran, J.L. (1976) 'Pupils' Perceptions in High and Low Delinquency Schools.' *Educational Research, 18*, 138-44.

Fix, A.J. and Haffke, E.A. (1976) *Basic Psychological Therapies: Comparative Effectiveness*. New York: Human Sciences Press.

Ford, J. (1969) *Social Class and the Comprehensive School*. London: Routledge & Kegan Paul.

Galloway, D.M. (1976) 'Persistent Unjustified Absence from School.' *Trends in Education, 4*, 22

Galloway, D.M. (1976) 'Size of School, Socio-economic Hardship, Suspension Rates and Persistent Unjustified Absence from School.' *British Journal of Educational Psychology, 46*, 40-7.

Galloway, D.M. (1977) 'Application of Behavioural Analysis and Behaviour Modification in School Psychological Service Practice.' *Bulletin of the British Association for Behavioural Psychotherapy, 5*, 63-6.

Galloway, D.M. (1980a) 'Exclusion and Suspension from School.' *Trends in Education*, (in press).

Galloway, D.M. (1980b) *Teaching and Counselling*. London: Longman.

Galloway, D.M. and Goodwin, C.A. (1979) *Educating Slow Learning and Maladjusted Children: Integration or Segregation*. London: Longman.

Galton, M., Simon, B. and Croll, P. (1980) *Inside the Primary School*. London: Routledge & Kegan Paul.

Gath, D., Cooper, B. and Gattoni, F.E.G. (1972) 'Child Guidance and Delinquency in a London Borough: Preliminary Communication.' *Psychological Medicine, 2*, 185-91.

Gath, D., Cooper, B., Gattoni, F. and Rockett, D. (1977) *Child Guidance and Delinquency in a London Borough*. Oxford: Oxford University Press.

Gillham, B. (1978) 'The Failure of Psychometrics', in B. Gillham (ed.) *Reconstructing Educational Psychology*. London: Croom Helm.

Gillham, B. (1980) 'Psychological Services and Problems of Adolescent Behaviour', in A. Gobell and G. Upton (eds) *The Challenge of Adolescent Behaviour in Schools*. University College, Cardiff: School of Education Occasional Publication.

Gilliland, J. (1972) *Readability*. London: Hodder & Stoughton.

Glen, F. (1975) *The Social Psychology of Organisations*. London: Methuen.

Goffman, E. (1961) *Asylums*. Harmondsworth: Penguin Books.

Goldstein, H. (1980) '*Fifteen Thousand Hours*: a Review of the Statistical Procedures.' *Journal of Child Psychology and Child Psychiatry*, (in press).

Goodman, S.M. (1959) *The Assessment of School Quality*. Albany: New York.

Gregory, P. (1980) 'Truancy: a Plan for School-based Action Research.' *Journal of the Association of Educational Psychologists, 5,* 3, 30-5.

Haigh, G. (1976) *The Reluctant Adolescent.* London: Temple Smith.

Halsey, A.H. (1980) 'Education Can Compensate.' *New Society,* 24 January.

Hanushek, E. (1972) *Education and Race.* Lexington, Mass: D.C. Heath.

Hargreaves, D.H. (1967) *Social Relationships in a Secondary School.* London: Routledge & Kegan Paul.

Hargreaves, D.H. (1978a) 'The Proper Study of Educational Psychology.' *Journal of the Association of Educational Psychologists, 4,* 9, 3-8.

Hargreaves, D.H. (1978b) 'Deviance: the Interactionist Approach', in B. Gillham (ed.) *Reconstructing Educational Psychology.* London: Croom Helm.

Hargreaves, D.H. (1980) 'Review of *Fifteen Thousand Hours.*' *British Journal of Sociology of Education, 1,* 211-16.

Hargreaves, D.H., Hestor, S. and Mellor, F.J. (1975) *Deviance in Classrooms.* London: Routledge & Kegan Paul.

Her Majesty's Inspectorate (1978a) *Truancy and Behaviour Problems in some Urban Schools.* London: Department of Education and Science.

Her Majesty's Inspectorate (1978b) *Behavioural Units: A Survey of Special Units for Pupils with Behavioural Problems.* London: Department of Education and Science.

Her Majesty's Inspectorate (1980) Report on a survey of Community Homes with Education. *Matters for Discussion Series.*

Hodgson, G. (1973) 'Inequality: Do Schools Make a Difference?' *Atlantic Monthly,* July.

Home Office (1979a) *Report on the Work of the Prison Department 1978.* London: HMSO.

Home Office (1979b) *Criminal Statistics for England and Wales 1978.* London: HMSO.

Hurn, C. (1978) *The Limits and Possibilities of Schooling.* Boston: Allyn & Bacon.

Husen, T. (1979) *The School in Question.* Oxford: Oxford University Press.

Illich, I. (1971) *Celebration of Awareness.* London: Calder & Boyars.

Illich, I. (1977) *Limits to Medicine.* Harmondsworth: Penguin Books.

Jencks, C. *et al.* (1972) *Inequality: A Reassessment of the Effect of Family and Schooling in America.* New York: Basic Books.

Jenkins, G.M. (1976) 'The Systems Approach', in J. Beishon and G. Peters (eds) *Systems Behaviour.* (2nd edition) London: Harper & Row.

Jensen, A. (1971) 'How Much Can We Boost IQ and Scholastic Attainment?' *Harvard Educational Review, 39,* 1-123.

Jones-Davies, C. and Cave, R. (eds) (1977) *The Disruptive Pupil in the Secondary School.* London: Ward Lock Educational.

Kast, F.E. and Rosenzweig, J.E. (1976) 'The modern view: a systems approach,' in J. Beishon and G. Peters (eds) *Systems Behaviour.* (2nd edition) London: Harper & Row.

Kounin, J.S., Friesen, W.V. and Norton, E. (1966) 'Managing Emotionally Disturbed Children in Regular Classrooms.' *Journal of Educational Psychology, 57,* 1-13.

Lacey, C. (1970) *Hightown Grammar: The School as a Social System.* Manchester: Manchester University Press.

Lambert, R., Bullock, R. and Millham, S. (1970) *A Manual of the Sociology of the School.* London: Weidenfeld & Nicolson.

Lane, D. (1976) 'Limitations on Counselling.' *Remedial Education, 11,* 3, 120.

Lane, D. (1978) *The Impossible Child.* London: ILEA.

Lemert, E.M. (1967) *Human Deviance: Social Problems and Social Control.* Englewood Cliffs: Prentice Hall.

Levitt, E.E. (1957) 'The Results of Psychotherapy With Children: an Evaluation.' *Journal of Consulting Psychology, 21,* 189-96.

Levitt, E.E. (1963) 'Psychotherapy With Children: a Further Evaluation.' *Behavior*

Research and Therapy, 1, 45-51.

Levitt, E.E. (1971) 'Research on Psychotherapy With Children,' in A.E. Bergin and S.L. Garfield (eds) *Handbook of Psychotherapy and Behaviour Change*. London: John Wiley.

Lindsay, G.A. (1980) 'The Infant-rating Schedule.' *British Journal of Educational Psychology*, (in press).

London Boroughs Children's Regional Planning Committee (1979) *Manpower and Training Needs of Community Homes with Education.* (unpublished report).

Long, N. and Newman, R. (1961) 'Managing Surface Behavior in Children.' *Bulletin of the School of Education, Indiana University.*

Madden, J.V. *et al.* (1976) *School Effectiveness Study.* State of California.

Marland, M. (1975) *The Craft of the Classroom: A Survival Guide.* London: Heinemann Educational.

Maughan, B. *et al.* (1980) '*Fifteen Thousand Hours*: a Reply to Heath and Clifford.' *Oxford Educational Review*, (in press).

Mayhew, P., Clarke, R.V.G., Sturman, A. and Hough, J.M. (1975) *Crime as Opportunity.* Home Office Research Study No. 34. London: HMSO.

McDill, B. *et al.* (1967) 'Institutional effects on the Academic Behavior of High School Students.' *Sociology of Education, 40*, 181-99.

McDill, B. *et al.* (1972) *Structure and Process in Secondary Schools.* Baltimore: Johns Hopkins University Press.

McFie, B.S. (1934) 'Behaviour and Personality Difficulties in School Children.' *British Journal of Educational Psychology, 4*, 30-46.

Merton, R.K. (1957) *Social Theory and Social Structure.* Glencoe, Ill.: Glencoe Free Press.

Metropolitan Police (1979) *Juvenile Bureau Statistics.* (Personal communication). Metropolitan Police: Communications Branch.

Miller, A. (1980) 'Systems Theory Applied to the Work of an Educational Psychologist.' *Journal of the Association of Educational Psychologists, 5*, 3, 11-16.

Millham, S., Bullock, R. and Cherrett, P. (1975) *After Grace – Teeth.* London: Human Content Books.

Millham, S., Bullock, R. and Hosie, K. (1978) *Locking Up Children.* Hampshire: Saxon House.

Milner, M. (1938) *The Human Problem in Schools.* London: Methuen.

Morris, A. (1978) 'Diversion of Juvenile Offenders from the Criminal Justice System,' in N. Tutt (ed.) *Alternative Strategies for Coping with Crime.* Oxford: Basil Blackwell.

Musgrave, P.W. (1968) *The School as an Organisation.* London: Macmillan.

Mycroft, D. (1978) *The Finsbury Unit.* Unpublished report: ILEA.

Mungham, G. and Pearson, G. (1976) *Working Class Youth Culture.* London: Routledge & Kegan Paul.

Newman, O. (1972) *Defensible Space: People and Design in the Violent City.* London: Architectural Press.

News Report (1971) 'Secondary School Crisis.' *Times Educational Supplement*, 8 October.

News Report (1979) 'Government to be Tough with Young Offenders.' Report of the Police Federation Annual Conference. *Guardian*, 17 May.

New York State Office of Education (1974) *School Factors Influencing Reading Attainment: A Case Study of Two Inner City Schools.*

Ouston, J., Maughan, B. and Mortimore, P. (1980) 'School Influence on Children's Development', in M. Rutter (ed.) *Scientific Foundation of Child Psychiatry.* London: Heinemann.

Partridge, J. (1966) *Life in a Secondary Modern School.* Harmondsworth: Penguin Books.

Peaker, G.F. (1967) 'The Regression Analysis of the National Survey', in *Children and their Primary Schools, Volume 2*. London: HMSO.

Pearson, G. (1976) 'In Defence of Hooliganism: Social Theory and Violence', in N.S. Tutt (ed.) *Violence*. London: HMSO.

Personal communication (1977) *Orders made in care proceedings under Section 1 of the Children's and Young Persons Act (1969)*. London: DHSS.

Phillipson, C.M. (1971) 'Juvenile Delinquency and the School', in W.G. Carson and P. Wiles (eds) *Crime and Delinquency in Britain*. London: Martin Robertson.

Power, M.J. *et al.* (1967) 'Delinquent Schools?' *New Society*, 19 October.

Power, M.J. *et al.* (1972) 'Neighbourhood, School and Juveniles Before the Courts.' *British Journal of Criminology, 12*, 111-32.

Quicke, J.C. (1976) 'Behavourism and Education: a Critique.' *Journal of the Association of Educational Psychologists, 3*, 8, 8-16.

Rabinowitz, A. (1977) 'Children and Their Difficulties in School.' Unpublished discussion paper. London: ILEA.

Rapopart, A. and Horvath, W. (1959) 'Thoughts on Organization Theory.' *General Systems, 4*, 87-91.

Raven, J. (1979) 'School Rejection and its Amelioration.' *Educational Research, 20*, 1.

Reade, A.W. (1971) *Indications Arising from a Study of High and Low Delinquency Rate Schools*. Unpublished study (cited by Gath *et al.*, 1977.)

Reynolds, D. (1975) 'When Teachers and Pupils Refuse a Truce', in G. Mungham (ed.) *Working Class Youth Culture*. London: Routledge & Kegan Paul.

Reynolds, D. (1976) 'The Delinquent School', in M. Hammersley and P. Woods (eds) *The Process of Schooling*. London: Routledge & Kegan Paul.

Reynolds, D. *et al.* (1976) 'Schools Do Make a Difference.' *New Society*, 29 July.

Reynolds, D. and Murgatroyd, S. (1977) 'The Sociology of Schooling and the Absent Pupil: the School as a Factor in the Generation of Truancy', in H.C.M. Carroll (ed.) *Absenteeism in South Wales: Studies of Pupils, their Homes and their Secondary Schools*. Swansea: Faculty of Education, University of Swansea.

Reynolds, D. and Jones, D. (1978) 'Education and the Prevention of Juvenile Delinquency', in N.S. Tutt (ed.) *Alternative Strategies for Coping with Crime*. Oxford: Basil Blackwell.

Reynolds, D. and Sullivan, M. (1979) 'Bringing Schools Back In', in L.A. Barton (ed.) *Schools, Pupils and Deviance*. Driffield: Nafferton.

Reynolds, D., Jones, D., St. Leger, S. and Murgatroyd, S. (1981) *Bringing Schools Back In*. London: Routledge & Kegan Paul.

Rice, A.K. (1963) *The Enterprise and its Environment*. London: Tavistock.

Rice, A.K. and Miller, E.J. (1967) *Systems of Organization*. London: Tavistock.

Richardson, E. (1973) *The Teacher, the School and the Task of Management*. London: Heinemann.

Robins, L.N. (1970) 'Follow-up studies investigating childhood disorders', in E.H. Hare and J.K. Wing (eds) *Psychiatric Epidemiology*. Oxford: Oxford University Press.

Rutter, M. (1965) 'Classification and Categorisation in Child Psychiatry.' *Journal of Child Psychology and Child Psychiatry, 6*, 71-83.

Rutter, M. (1972) Critical notice: M. Shepherd, B. Oppenheim and S. Mitchell (1971) *Childhood Behaviour and Mental Health*. London: University of London Press. *Journal of Child Psychology and Child Psychiatry, 13*, 219-22.

Rutter, M. (1973) 'Why are London Children So Disturbed?' *Proceedings of the Royal Society of Medicine, 66*, 1221-5.

Rutter, M. (1980) *Changing Youth in a Changing World*. London: Nuffield Provincial Hospitals Trust.

190   *References*

Rutter, M., Tizard, J. and Whitmore, K. (1970) *Education, Health and Behaviour.*
London: Longman.
Rutter, M. and Madge, N. (1976) *Cycles of Disadvantage.* London: Heinemann.
Rutter, M., Maughan, B., Mortimore, P. and Ouston, J. (1979) *Fifteen Thousand Hours: Secondary Schools and their Effects on Children.* London: Open Books.
Schools Council (1973) *Evaluation in Curriculum Development: Twelve Studies.*
London: Macmillan.
Shaycroft, M. (1967) *The High School Years: Growth in Cognitive Skills.*
Pittsburgh: American Institute for Research in Education.
Shepherd, M., Oppenheim, B. and Mitchell, S. (1971) *Childhood Behaviour and Mental Health.* London: University of London Press.
Shipman, M. (1968) *The Sociology of the School.* London: Longman.
Shipman, M. (1979) *In-school Evaluation.* London: Heinemann.
Skemp, R.R. (1979) *Intelligence, Learning and Action.* Chichester: John Wiley.
Steedman, J. (1980) *Progress in Secondary Education.* London: National Children's Bureau.
Stenhouse, L. (1980) *Curriculum Research and Development.* London: Heinemann.
Stephens, J.M. (1967) *The Process of Schooling.* New York: John Wiley.
Stephenson, G. (1981) 'Individuals and the Social System: The case of authoritarianism', in C.I. Howarth and W.E.C. Gillham (eds) *The Structure of Psychology.* London: George Allen & Unwin.
Stott, D.M. (1975) *Taxonomy of Behaviour Disturbance.* London: University of London Press.
Stufflebeam, D.L. (1969) 'Toward a Science of Educational Evaluation.' *Educational Technology, 8,* 14, 5-12.
Sutton, A. (1978) 'Theory, Practice, and Cost in Child Care: Implications from an Individual Case.' *Howard League Journal, 16,* 3, 159-71.
Taylor, A. (1979) 'Contract-based School Work – its Rationale, Practice and Evaluation.' *Journal of the Association of Educational Psychologists, 5,* 1, 21-5.
Tizard, J. (1973) 'Maladjusted Children and the Child Guidance Service.' *London Educational Review, 2,* 2, 22-37.
Tizard, J. (1976) 'Psychology and Social Policy.' *Bulletin of the British Psychological Society, 29,* 225-34.
Topping, K.J. (1978) 'Consumer Confusion and Professional Conflict in Educational Psychology.' *Bulletin of the British Psychological Society, 31,* 265-7.
Topping, K. (1979) 'The Psychology of Organisations.' *Journal of the Association of Educational Psychologists, 5,* 1, 2-4.
Topping, K. and Quelch, T. (1976) *Special Units and Classes for Children with Behaviour Problems.* Calderdale Education Department.
Tulkens, H. (1979) *Some Developments in Penal Policy and Practice in Holland.*
London: NACRO.
Tunley, P., Travers, T. and Pratt, J. (1980) *Depriving the Deprived.* London: Kogan.
Tutt, N.S. (1974) *Care or Custody.* London: Darton, Longman & Todd.
Tutt, N.S. (1975) *Care or Control.* Birmingham: Movement of Practising Psychologists, Discussion Paper No. 5.
Tutt, N.S. (1976) In: *Observation and Assessment: A Changing Concept.* Birmingham: Selly Oak Colleges.
Tutt, N.S. (1977) 'Use and Development of Observation and Assessment Centres for Children.' *Report of a joint ADSS/SWS seminar.* London: DHSS.
Tutt, N.S. (1978) 'Delinquency – Social Workers' Changing Role.' *Social Work Today, 9,* 30.

Ullman, L.P. and Krasner, L. (1975) *A Psychological Approach to Abnormal Behaviour.* (2nd edition) Englewood Cliffs: Prentice-Hall.

Ward, J. (1976) 'Behaviour Modification in Education: an Overview and a Model for Planned Implementation.' *Bulletin of the British Psychological Society, 29,* 257-68.

Weber, G. (1971) *Inner City Children can be Taught to Read: Four Successful Schools.* Washington D.C.: Council for Basic Education.

Werthman, C. (1963) 'Delinquents in Schools: a Test for the Legitimacy of Authority.' *Berkeley Journal of Sociology, 8,* 39-60.

West, D.J. and Farrington, D.P. (1973) *Who Becomes Delinquent?* London: Heinemann.

West, D. and Farrington, D.P. (1977) *The Delinquent Way of Life.* London: Heinemann.

Westergaard, J. and Reisler, H. (1975) *Class in a Capitalist Society.* London: Heinemann.

Whiteside, T. (1978) *The Sociology of Educational Innovation.* London: Methuen.

Wilby, P. (1977) 'Education and Equality.' *New Statesman,* 16 September.

Wilson, M. and Evans, M. (1979) 'Special Units for Disturbed or Disruptive Pupils.' *Contact,* London: ILEA.

Wolff, S. (1976) 'Non-delinquent Disturbance of Conduct', in M. Rutter and L. Hersov (eds) *Child Psychiatry.* Oxford: Basil Blackwell.

Wright, D.M., Moelis, I. and Pollack, L.J. (1976) 'The Outcome of Individual Child Psychotherapy: Increments at Follow-up.' *Journal of Child Psychology and Child Psychiatry, 17,* 275-85.

Zimmerman, E.H. and Zimmerman, J. (1962) 'The Alteration of Behavior in a Special Classroom Situation.' *Journal for the Experimental Analysis of Behavior, 51,* 59-60.

NOTES ON CONTRIBUTORS

Bill Gillham Tutor to the MA course in Child and Educational Psychology, University of Nottingham

Robert Burden Tutor to the MEd course in Educational Psychology, University of Exeter

David Reynolds Lecturer in Social Administration, University College, Cardiff

Michael Sullivan Research Fellow, Department of Social Administration, University College, Cardiff

Janet Ouston Research Fellow, Institute of Psychiatry, London

Arno Rabinowitz Deputy Principal Educational Psychologist, ILEA

Norman Tutt Professor of Applied Social Studies, University of Lancaster

Robert Daines Educational Psychologist, East Sussex School Psychological Service

John Hastings Headmaster, Glaisdale Comprehensive School, Nottingham

Robert Pik Educational Psychologist, Solihull School Psychological Service

Joan Figg Educational Psychologist, Nottinghamshire School Psychological Service

Andrew Ross Educational Psychologist, Nottinghamshire School Psychological Service

David Galloway Senior Lecturer in Education, Victoria University of Wellington, New Zealand (formerly Senior Educational Psychologist, Sheffield)

INDEX